Corporate Citizenship and Family Business

Current models of corporate citizenship largely consider business as one coherent entity. This view of business as a corporate force overlooks the growing evidence that most businesses are run by families. Family businesses are the most common form of business in existence – across countries, continents, and geopolitical divides – and yet we know remarkably little about their approach to corporate citizenship. Where families run businesses, they create a concentration of family values that – for good or ill – influence the way business practices and behaviours develop.

The role of the family in business has, therefore, an influence on the development of society that is partially mediated through corporate citizenship. This book pulls together current thinking from several diverse research fields that intersect with family business research to offer insight into current research and examples of practice for those studying and researching in the fields of family business, business values, and corporate practice. The book will also explore the fact that family businesses tend to take a longer-term approach to business and that this is reflected in their behaviour towards the environment, community engagement, employee development, and innovation.

Bringing together contributions from researchers in the diverse fields of family business, philanthropy, community engagement, corporate social responsibility, innovation and policy, this book explores the many ways in which family businesses contribute to the corporate citizenship agenda.

Claire Seaman holds the Chair in Enterprise and Family Business at Queen Margaret University in Edinburgh, UK. She is Editor in Chief for the Journal of Family Business Management.

Citizenship and Sustainability in Organizations
Series Editors: David F Murphy and Alison Marshall

Exploring how organizations and citizens respond to and influence current and future global transformations, this book series publishes excellent, innovative and critical scholarship in the fields of citizenship, social responsibility, sustainability, innovation, and place leadership in diverse organizational contexts. These contexts include commercial businesses, social enterprises, public service organizations, international organizations, faith-based organizations (FBOs), non-governmental organizations (NGOs), community groups, hybrids, and cross-sector partnerships. The role of the individual as a citizen may also be explored in relation to one or more of these contexts, as could formal or informal networks, clusters and organizational ecosystems.

The Intelligent Nation: How to Organise a Country
John Beckford

Citizenship and Sustainability in Organizations
Exploring and Spanning the Boundaries
Edited by David F. Murphy and Alison Marshall

Knowledge Management and Sustainability
A Human-Centered Perspective on Research and Practice
Edited by David Israel Contreras-Medina, Julia Pérez Bravo and Elia Socorro Díaz Nieto

Corporate Citizenship and Family Business
Edited by Professor Claire Seaman

Corporate Citizenship and Family Business

Edited by Claire Seaman

LONDON AND NEW YORK

First published 2022
by Routledge
4 Park Square, Milton Park, Abingdon, Oxon OX14 4RN

and by Routledge
605 Third Avenue, New York, NY 10158

Routledge is an imprint of the Taylor & Francis Group, an informa business

© 2022 selection and editorial matter, Claire Seaman; individual chapters, the contributors

The right of Claire Seaman to be identified as the author of the editorial material, and of the authors for their individual chapters, has been asserted in accordance with sections 77 and 78 of the Copyright, Designs and Patents Act 1988.

All rights reserved. No part of this book may be reprinted or reproduced or utilised in any form or by any electronic, mechanical, or other means, now known or hereafter invented, including photocopying and recording, or in any information storage or retrieval system, without permission in writing from the publishers.

Trademark notice: Product or corporate names may be trademarks or registered trademarks, and are used only for identification and explanation without intent to infringe.

British Library Cataloguing-in-Publication Data
A catalogue record for this book is available from the British Library

Library of Congress Cataloging-in-Publication Data
A catalog record has been requested for this book

ISBN: 978-0-367-23703-5 (hbk)
ISBN: 978-1-032-24776-2 (pbk)
ISBN: 978-0-429-28122-8 (ebk)

DOI: 10.4324/9780429281228

Typeset in Sabon
by MPS Limited, Dehradun

Contents

List of Contributors		vii
Introduction CLAIRE SEAMAN		1
1	Citizenship Behaviours in Family Enterprises: Understanding Its Nature and Dimensionality NEUS FELIU AND ISABEL C. BOTERO	8
2	Sustainability in Historic Family Firms ANNE BARRAQUIER	34
3	Employees Returns on "Ramadan Packages" as a Corporate Social Responsibility Practice: Moderating Role of Perceived Corporate Sincerity ERHAN BOĞAN	56
4	Antecedents and Influences of Corporate Citizenship: Case Study of a Finnish Family Firm AHMAD ARSLAN, PIA HURMELINNA-LAUKKANEN, LAURI HAAPANEN, AND DEBORAH CALLAGHAN	70
5	Family Businesses, Family Values and Corporate Citizenship PAROMA SEN AND IPSHITA ADHIKARY	85
6	Does Corporate Citizenship Have Gender? AMALIA VERDU SANMARTIN	102

vi *Contents*

7 Impact of Financial and Cost Management
Systems for Family-Owned Businesses'
Corporate Citizenship 114
PADMI NAGIRIKANDALAGE AND ARNAZ BINSARDI

8 Consciously Contributing: Community
Engagement, Philanthropy and Family Business 123
CLAIRE SEAMAN AND RICHARD BENT

Index 133

Contributors

Professor Claire Seaman holds the Chair in Enterprise and Family Business at Queen Margaret University in Edinburgh. Her research focuses on family businesses, startups and scaleup businesses in Scotland and worldwide. She is Editor in Chief for the Journal of Family Business Management.

Dr Neus Feliu is a consultant, researcher, and educator in the area of family enterprises. She is a partner at Lansberg Gersick and Associates. Building on her background in economics and organizational psychology, she has developed an expertise in the governance, long-term sustainability planning, and ownership strategies of family enterprise. Neus obtained her PhD from ESADE Business School.

Isabel C. Botero, Ph.D., is the Director of the Family Business Center and an associate professor of entrepreneurship at the University of Louisville. She is a Fellow for the Family Firm Institute and has an Advanced Certificate in Family Wealth Advising. Her research focuses on strategic communication processes, governance, and next-generation issues in family enterprises. She is an associate editor for the journal of family business strategy and a past FOBI Scholar. Her work has been published in multiple management, communication, and family business books and journals.

Anne Barraquier is a lecturer at SKEMA Business School, in France. Her research looks at the micro-foundations of sustainability in business (British Journal of Management, Journal of Business Ethics, and others). Prior to academia, she worked as an international trade manager in Hong Kong and a strategy consultant in France.

Erhan Boğan, PhD, is currently working as Associate Professor in Faculty of Tourism at Adıyaman University/Turkey. He published articles in top-tier journals as International Journal of Hospitality Management and Journal of Hospitality Marketing and Management. His research interests include corporate social responsibility, behavioural integrity, Islamic tourism, and halal tourism.

viii *Contributors*

Dr Ahmad Arslan is currently working as Associate Professor (Senior Research Fellow) at Oulu Business School, University of Oulu, Finland. He also holds the position of Honorary Chair (Professor) at the Business School, University of Aberdeen, Scotland, UK. He has multidisciplinary research interests in different areas of management sciences. His earlier research has been published in prestigious academic journals like the British Journal of Management, Human Resource Management (US), International Business Review, International Marketing Review, Journal of Business Research, and Technological Forecasting and Social Change among others. Moreover, he has also contributed book chapters to several books addressing different management-related topics. He holds several editorial board memberships and is currently a Senior Editor of the International Journal of Emerging Markets (Emerald).

Dr Pia Hurmelinna is a Professor of Marketing, especially International Business. She has published about 75 refereed articles in journals such as Journal of Product Innovation Management, Industrial and Corporate Change, and International Business Research. Her research involves topics around innovation and covers contexts like networks and internationalization.

Lauri Haapanen is Assistant Professor of International Business at the Oulu Business School, Finland. With more than 20 years of experience in managing international firms, his main research interests reside in internationally expanding firms' key functions, particularly in the interplay between R&D, sales & marketing, and the top management.

Dr Deborah Callaghan is a Senior Lecturer in Human Resource Management and Organisational Behaviour at Liverpool John Moores University. Deborah has taught international business strategy, social responsibility, OB and CIPD (inter)nationally accredited HRM programmes. Her research interests include contemporary labour market challenges, business ethics, and workplace bullying and harassment.

Dr Paroma Sen, PhD, is currently an independent researcher with four years of experience of teaching Public Policy and Public Administration in Lady Shri Ram College for Women, University of Delhi. She enjoys reading, writing, and travelling. She is presently working on the issue of emotional labour in a post-pandemic world.

Ipshita Adhikary is a Political Science/Economics graduate from Lady Shri Ram College who chose to study business. I now work in the Human Resources department in the retail sector. Her hobbies include reading and moving weights in the gym.

Contributors ix

Amalia Verdu Sanmartin, PhD in Law, is a postdoctoral researcher at the Turku Institution for Advance Studies (TIAS). She does interdisciplinary research with a focus on discrimination, teaching methods, legal knowledge and legal subjects.

Dr Padmi Nagirikandalage is a Senior Lecturer in Accounting and Finance at Nottingham Trent University. She completed her UG and PG studies at the University of Colombo, Sri Lanka. She then obtained a PhD in Accounting and Finance from the University of Wales, UK. Her expertise: Accounting, Finance, and Research Methodology.

Dr Arnaz Binsardi is a Reader at Glyndwr University. He completed his UG and PG studies at Texas Tech and Wichita State Universities. He then obtained a PhD from Loughborough University, studying econometrics and undertook a Research Fellowship at the University of Oxford. His expertise is in research methodology, accounting, and econometrics.

Richard Bent is Senior Lecturer in Management at Queen Margaret University, Edinburgh specializing in smaller and family enterprises. He has published numerous journal articles in the areas of SME, family businesses and retail, with regular presentations at a range of International and UK Conferences. A regular contributor to BBC Radio Scotland programmes in the areas of topical consumer and retail issues. Involvement in consultancy work through a wide range of Innovation projects ensures that his teaching and interaction with business and business support agencies are kept rooted in both practical realities and theory. An additional interest in the areas of theme parks.

Introduction

Claire Seaman

This book starts from the precept that 'society' is largely created by three key dimensions that intersect: Government, business, and the community organisations that make up what is commonly referred to as 'civil society', operating in the natural environment (Waddell, 2016). Whilst individuals certainly play a part, the collective power of these three dimensions shape the behaviour of individuals and indeed the families and societies in which we live. Within current models, however, business is largely considered as one coherent entity. This view of business as a corporate force overlooks the growing evidence that most businesses are run by families. Where families run businesses, they create a concentration of family values that – for good or ill – influence the way business practices and behaviours develop. The role of the family in business has, therefore, an influence on the development of society that is partially mediated through corporate citizenship. Further study of the way family businesses act as corporate citizens is therefore merited and this book pulls together current thinking from several diverse research fields that intersect with family business research. As a prelude, however, an overview of the role of family business is merited.

Family businesses are the most common form of business in existence, across countries, continents, and geopolitical divides, yet we know remarkably little about their approach to corporate citizenship. The importance of family businesses, in economic terms, has been researched worldwide and the conclusion established that family businesses form a cornerstone of the economies of most developed countries and appear to provide a degree of community and social stability [Poutziouris, 2006; Kets de Vries and Carlock, 2007 pxiii; Institute for Family Business, 2009]. Estimates of the predominance of family business vary, in part due to a lack of definitional clarity, but numerous authors have estimated that somewhere between 65% and 80% of businesses have families at the core of the business (Collins *et al.*, 2010; Collins *et al.*, 2010; Seaman, 2012, Seaman *et al.*, 2015, 2016). This definitional debate merits further discussion within the family business research community, but in the context of corporate citizenship the definitional challenges are

DOI: 10.4324/9780429281228-1

2 Claire Seaman

probably less important than the precept that where a family controls a business, the values of that family will contribute to behaviour within that business and hence to corporate citizenship. There is also an increasing portfolio of research that suggests that family businesses behave differently from businesses without a substantive family component. Despite their economic importance, the family business is a relatively young field of research (Siebels and Knyphausen Aufseb, 2012) and their inclusion into mainstream business thinking in the field of corporate citizenship is timely. A variety of research also indicates that values influence business decision making and there is clear evidence that where one family has a predominant role in a business their collective values will play a strong role in guiding business behaviour. Similarly, research indicates that family businesses tend to take a longer-term approach to business and that this is reflected in their behaviour towards the environment, community engagement, employee development and indeed innovation. The impact that this, in turn, may have on the approach of family businesses to corporate citizenship is explored here.

Definitions of corporate citizenship also vary, but most include the idea that corporations, businesses or business-like organisations have a degree of social responsibility, that often includes a responsibility to the families of their employees. Theories that map the traditional territory of corporate social responsibility (Garriga and Melé, 2004) have developed a theory in this area, but far less attention has been paid to the scenario where the family is an integral part of the business (McIntosh *et al.*, 1998). Family businesses are astonishingly numerous, often underresearched and yet substantively involved in corporate citizenship, sometimes *via* formalized routes that include philanthropy and community engagement, but also through their business practices and approaches to corporate social responsibility. Attempts to place corporate citizenship within the literature that looks at business-society relations have not been altogether successful (Maten and Krane, 2005) and one reason may be that by overlooking the often less visible family dimension one driving force is, to some extent, overlooked. Factoring the family dimension into current corporate citizenship research and the developing potential for new work in this area has the potential to shed light on hitherto unexplored aspects of corporate governance.

Starting from the precept that businesses do sometimes behave as citizens or citizen groups and that their behaviour is important to the longer-term environment in economic, social, and environmental terms, this book seeks to explore the many ways in which family businesses contribute to the corporate citizenship agenda. Pulling together work from writers in the diverse fields of family business, philanthropy, community engagement, corporate social responsibility, innovation and policy, an overview is developed of current knowledge and highlights areas of interest for future research. Family Business is a relatively young field of research where there

Introduction 3

is scope for considerable additional development and this book seeks to consider what is already known, alongside the policy options available and the development of a research agenda in this field.

Corporate citizenship is defined in many ways, but most definitions include the idea that corporations, businesses or business-like organisations have a degree of social responsibility, that often includes communities, causes, staff and indeed the families of their employees. Far less attention focuses on the scenario where the family is an integral part of the business. Family businesses are astonishingly numerous, often underresearched and yet substantively involved in corporate citizenship, via formalized philanthropy and community engagement, but also through their business practices and approaches to corporate social responsibility. Indeed, family businesses form a cornerstone of economies worldwide, operating across countries, continents and geopolitical frontiers, yet family business represents a relatively young field of study. The implications of family ownership and indeed management for corporate citizenship remain relatively unexplored. Two factors may combine here; family businesses are numerically dominant in most societies. Definitions vary, but somewhere between 65% and 80% of businesses are 'family businesses'; an estimate that emerges as a consensus from the literature despite the ongoing definitional debate. Many, but by no means all, of these businesses fall into the 'SME' bracket, whilst a few will be larger, and the group includes both multi-national and multigenerational businesses. Similarly, family businesses operate across many different sectors of business and sectoral papers may offer unique insight into certain aspects of corporate citizenship. Family values are a sometimes-contentious topic, even within families themselves, and diverse views are often linked to concepts of tradition and behavioural expectations. In this chapter, we have chosen to pull together the opinions and contextualise them as being defined here as principles or standards of behaviour. Where the family run a business, family values take on much clearer dimensions and indeed have developed into an area of some considerable study, focussed on the way the values of the family influence business behaviour. Indeed, a recent report by PWC highlighted the common perception that the two defining, and distinguishing, characteristics of a family business are stewardship and heritage, often associated with a sense of duty towards the business. By managing the business assets and heritage, it is argued, values that may underpin business sustainability are distributed inter-generationally.

The following chapters aim, therefore, to highlight key aspects of the study that relate to business sustainability in its widest sense. We start, therefore, with a chapter that focuses on the nature and dimensionality of citizenship behaviours in family business. From the current body of research, much of which has developed in an organizational context, this chapter sets the scene and allows the reader a base from which to

4 Claire Seaman

consider some highly specific work at the intersection of family business and corporate citizenship research. This opening work is followed by a chapter focusing upon sustainability in historic family firms, whose research considers corporate social responsibility and family values intersect with the primary need to sustain the business as an economic entity. The historic perspective is especially useful here, as both corporate citizenship and sustainability are areas where the impact of business behaviours must be viewed as a long-term construct if sense is to be made of the effects of business and family behaviour. Definitions of family vary, however, and the historical context is an important area that presents some challenges for researchers. Social historians, anthropologists, and psychologists have described a wide variety of forms and norms for that entity described as 'family', over a wide variety of historical time periods and social settings (Seaman and Bent, 2017). Indeed, the word family is derived from the Latin 'familia, meaning 'household servants, family' and closely linked to famulus (servant). In more recent times, there is some evidence that the word 'family' was used to mean a group of slaves, but more recent commentary has reached general agreement that a family is:

> *'a group of individuals linked by blood, living arrangements, marriage or civil partnership who consider themselves to be family, who often choose to spend time together and may live together'.*
> Adapted from: Family: Business Dictionary (2016)

While the historical perspective is interesting, there are also a variety of different contexts where the word family is used in the 21st century, including the familial analogy in business (Seaman, 2012) and indeed varying social structures in countries where religion or tribal affiliation form a core societal unit. This definitional debate is critical, however, because it provides a backdrop to the understanding that family norms and values can only be fairly considered in the context of the time and place in which they are formulated (Bloch and Harrari, 1996) and lends weight to the ongoing discussion in the family business literature about the importance of context in family (Seaman and Bent, 2017). Family values, in turn, are defined here as:

> *'the principles and standards of behaviour, one's judgement of what is important in life'.*
> Oxford English Dictionary (2016)

An example follows in the following chapter, where the impact of 'Ramadan packages' is considered in the context of corporate social responsibility but, building on the 'values' theme, considers the moderating role of perceived corporate sincerity.

Introduction 5

The 'values' theme continues in the next chapter, where an alternative cultural perspective follows, in a case study of a Finnish family firm. Looking at the antecedents and influences of corporate citizenship this chapter offers an insight into the way in which corporate citizenship develops over time in a family business context. The role of family values is considered more explicitly in the following chapter which leads on to a consideration of gender in the context of family business and corporate citizenship behaviours. Focusing on the family within the business and the intersection with family research in a much wider sense, initially drawing on gender research to explore the evidence of a gender component within corporate citizenship. The historical idea that a 'citizen' was 'male' may influence current thinking on corporate citizenship and a feminist discourse on corporate citizenship offers an additional and useful perspective. The impact of corporate citizenship on the reputation of family firms forms the final chapter of this section, where Ahmad Arslan, Pia Hurmelinna-Laukkanen, Lauri Haapanen and Deborah Callaghan explore the antecedents and influences of corporate citizenship in family firms operating n the medical supplies sector. A view of business behaviour through the lens of the perceived impact on business reputation offers the reader the opportunity to focus on who the business (or indeed the family behind the business) perceive themselves to be and how they want their own and their business behaviour to be seen by the World.

The economic imperative forms the focus of the next chapter, where the impact of financial and cost management systems in the family business on their corporate citizenship behaviours is considered. This leads naturally to the final chapter, which looks at the extent to which the decision to contribute to local economies and communities is a conscious choice. In doing so, it touches on both formalized philanthropy and community engagement. The distinction between philanthropy and community engagement, also referred to in places as corporate community engagement or corporate community involvement or indeed corporate community investment, is often somewhat artificial, but where philanthropy generally refers to monitory gifting, community engagement is often on a much smaller scale. This does not imply that community engagement is less important: the local business that supports the local children's football team plays a role commensurate with the business size and contributes to social and community cohesion in a very distinct way. This final section of the book considers evidence around family businesses that consciously contribute through either philanthropy or community giving and the contribution they make to society. Contributed by Claire Seaman and Richard Bent, the chapter ends with the development of an early-stage research agenda highlighting areas where future research would help to explore the impact of family businesses on philanthropy, community engagement and indeed the

6 Claire Seaman

wider field of corporate citizenship. Family business is a relatively young field of research and there is considerable potential to bring forward work in the future that illuminates the contribution of this diverse, heterogeneous and incredibly numerous group of businesses.

References

Blodget, M.S., Dumas, C. and Zanzi, A. (2011) 'Emerging trends in global ethics: A comparative study of U.S. and international family business values', *Journal of Business Ethics*, 99, pp. 29–38

Cater, C., Collins, L.A. and Brent, D.B. (2015) 'Family firm engagement in fair trade business models. United States Association for small business and entrepreneurship'. Conference Proceedings; Boca Raton: R1-R23. Boca Raton: United States Association for Small Business and Entrepreneurship.

Cennamo, C. *et al.* (2012) 'Socioemotional wealth and proactive stakeholder engagement: Why family-controlled firms care more about their stakeholders', *Entrepreneurship Theory and Practice*, 36, pp. 1153–1173. DOI: 10.1111/j.1540-6520.2012.00543.x

Collins, L. and O'Regan, N. (2010) 'The evolving field of family business', *Journal of Family Business Management*, 1(1), pp. 5–13. ISSN 2043-6238.

Collins, L., O'Regan, N., Hughes, T. and Tucker, J. (2010) 'Strategic thinking in family businesses', *Strategic Change*, 19(1–2), pp. 57–76. ISSN 1086-1718.

Deniz, M. de la Cruz and Suarez, M.K.C. (2005) 'Corporate social responsibility and family business in Spain', *Journal of Business Ethics*, 56, pp. 27–41.

Fletcher, D. (2002) 'Understanding the small family business', *Routledge Studies in Small Business*. London and New York: Taylor and Francis Group.

Garcia, M.E., Frunzi, K., Dean, C.B., Flores, N. and Miller, K.B. (2016) Toolkit of resources for engaging families and the community as partners in education. Part 1: Building an understanding of family and community engagement. *REL*, pp. 2016–2148 https://eric.ed.gov/?id=ED569110

Garriga, E. and Melé, D. (2004) 'Corporate social responsibility theories: Mapping the territory', *Journal of Business Ethics*, 53(1), pp. 51–71.

Hall, A. (2002) 'Towards an understanding of strategy processes in small family business', in D.E. Fletcher (ed.), *Understanding the Small Family Business*. London and New York: Routledge Studies in Small Business. Taylor and Francis Group.

Institute for Family Business (2009) 'Natural philanthropists: Findings of the family business philanthropy and social responsibility inquiry'. http://www.cgap.org.uk/uploads/natural-philanthropists.pdf

Kets de Vries, M.F.R. and Carlock, R.S. (2007) *Family Business on the Couch*. London: Wiley and Sons.

Maten, D. and Krane, A. (2005) 'Corporate citizenship: Toward aqn extended theoretical conceptualisation,' *Academy of Management Review*, 30(1), pp. 166–179

McIntosh, M., Leipziger, D., Jones, K. and Coleman, G. (1998). *Corporate citizenship: Successful strategies for responsible companies*. London, UK: Pitman Publishing.

Poutziouris, Z.P. (2006) The structure and performance of the UK family business PLC economy, in Poutziouris P.Z., Smyrnios K.X. and Klein S.B. (eds.), *Handbook of research on family businesses*. Cheltenham, UK: Edward Elgar.

Seaman, C. and Bent, R. (2017) 'The role of family values in the integrity of family business', in Orlitzky M. and Monga Manjit (eds.), *Facets of integrity in business and management*. Routledge.

Seaman, C., Bent, R. and Unis, A. (2016) 'The role of context. South Asian family firms in Scotland and the Succession Paradox', *International Journal of Management Practice. Special Issue on 'The Role of Context in Family Firms'*, 9(4), pp. 433–437.

Seaman, C., Bent, R. and Unis, A. (2015) The Future of Family Entrepreneurship: Family Culture, Education and Entrepreneurial Intent in Scottish Pakistani Communities. Futures. Special Issue on the Futures of Family Entrepreneurship, in Randerson K., Fayolle A. and Bettinelli C. (eds.), http://www.sciencedirect.com/science/article/pii/S0016328715300458

Seaman, Claire (2013) 'The invisible bedrock: Business families, networks and the creation of entrepreneurial space', *World Review of Entrepreneurship, Management and Sustainable Development*, 9(1), pp. 101–113. ISSN 1746-0573.

Seaman, Claire (2012) 'The invisible bedrock: Four constructs of family business space', *World Review of Entrepreneurship, Management and Sustainable Development*, 8(3), pp. 297–307. ISSN 1746-0573.

Siebels, J. F. and Knyphausen Aufseb, D.Z. (2012) 'A review of theory in family business research: The implication for corporate governance', *International Journal of Management Reviews*, 14, pp. 280–304

Waddell, S. (2016) 'Core competences: A key force in business-government-civil society collaborations', in Mackintosh Malcolm (ed.), *Globalisation and corporate citizenship: The alternative gaze*. Sheffield: Greenleaf Publishing, pp. 19–22.

1 Citizenship Behaviours in Family Enterprises: Understanding Its Nature and Dimensionality

Neus Feliu and Isabel C. Botero

Introduction

In the organizational literature, the concept of citizenship has been used to describe behaviours of individuals and organizations that go beyond what is included as part of their responsibilities (Matten and Crane, 2005; Organ, 1997). At the individual level, the study of organizational citizenship behaviour has focused on understanding the drivers of these behaviours, the outcomes associated with individual citizenship behaviours, and the dimensionality of citizenship (LePine *et al.* 2002; Spitzmuller *et al.*, 2008). At the corporate level, research on citizenship has focused on articulating what corporate citizenship is, its drivers, and associated outcomes (Barnett and Salomon, 2012; Carroll, 1998; Matten and Crane, 2005). In an environment where stakeholders hold individuals and companies accountable for both their financial and social performance, the general perception is that citizenship behaviours are likely to result in positive outcomes for the individual (e.g. higher job satisfaction, higher commitment, better mental health) and the corporation (e.g. better reputation, more satisfied employees, and better financial performance). As a reflection of this, research understanding individual, group, and organizational citizenship has flourished, and has generated a lot of traction from practitioners and researchers.

Although citizenship behaviours have been explored in the general management literature, in the family business context, academic research in this area is just starting, and has primarily focused on understanding the behaviour at the corporate level. For example, Miller, Le Breton-Miller and Scholnick (2008) suggest that family enterprises may be more inclined to engage in corporate citizenship behaviours because they have more at stake than non-family firms. Binz Astrachan *et al.* (2017) complement this knowledge by presenting a conceptual model showing how family and business goals drive different aspects of corporate citizenship, and how engaging in corporate citizenship can influence the reputation and performance of the family enterprise. More recently,

DOI: 10.4324/9780429281228-2

Campopiano *et al.* (2019) explored the presence of women in the boards of directors as an important driver of corporate citizenship behaviours in family-controlled firms. However, even though family business scholars have highlighted that family firms are more likely to engage in corporate citizenship behaviours (Dyer and Whetten, 2006; Godfrey, 2005; Kashmiri and Mahajan, 2010; Seaman, 2017; Ward, 1997), we still have a very limited understanding of the nature and dimensionality of citizenship behaviours that occur in family enterprises (i.e. what are the different levels of citizenship behaviour?), and the drivers and outcomes associated with the dimensions of these behaviours. Understanding these aspects of family enterprise citizenship behaviours could help us outline the unique role that the business family might play in this behaviour and important areas that need to be explored in future research.

Building on previous work about citizenship behaviour at the corporate and individual level (Carroll, 1998; Graham, 1991; Matten and Crane, 2005; Organ, 1988), this chapter has four goals. First, we explain the concept of citizenship behaviour and outline what we know about citizenship behaviours in the context of family enterprises. Second, we propose a multi-level model to better understand the nature of citizenship behaviours within the family enterprise context. Third, we introduce the concept of business family citizenship and outline the drivers and outcomes associated with this type of citizenship behaviour within family enterprises. We finalize our chapter by the interconnections between the different levels of our model and outlining important areas for future research.

Citizenship Behaviours

The study of citizenship behaviours in the organizational context can be traced back to the work of Barnard (1938) and Katz (1964). Initially, the interest was centred on employee discretionary work behaviours that are not directly or explicitly recognized by the formal reward system of the organization but are important for its effective functioning (Organ, 1988). Later, this work shifted to include the behaviour of corporations that goes beyond profit-making to include the contributions of companies to the community and other important stakeholders (Carroll, 1979, 1998). However, the "citizenship" label was originally coined in the political philosophy literature to describe the status of belonging somewhere, and the responsibilities and rights that are associated with belonging (Graham 1986, 1991, 2000). Graham (1991) argues that citizens have three important responsibilities: Obedience (i.e. respect for orderly structures and processes), loyalty (i.e. concern for the welfare of others, the state, and the values that it embodies), and participation (i.e. involvement in governance). At the same time, citizens have civil (i.e. legal protection of life, liberty, and property), political (i.e. participation in

10 *Neus Feliu and Isabel C. Botero*

decision-making), and social rights (i.e. socioeconomic benefits) that are not available to noncitizens (Graham, 1991).

Building on this idea of citizenship, two parallel literatures developed within organizational research. On one hand, organizational behaviour scholars and social psychologists explore the idea of *organizational citizenship behaviours (OCBs)*. Research on OCBs has centred on understanding employee behaviours that are discretionary (i.e. a matter of personal choice) and contribute "to the maintenance and enhancement of the social and psychological context that supports task performance" (Organ, 1997, p. 91). This area of citizenship behaviours has received a lot of attention from scholars who have tried to articulate the factors that drive employee OCBs, the different types of OCBs that occur in an organization, and the different types of outcomes that are affected by these behaviours (Spitzmuller *et al.*, 2008). Although there have been many types of OCBs explored (See: Ilies *et al.*, 2007; LePine *et al.*, 2002; Podsakoff *et al.*, 2009 for detailed lists), these behaviours can be grouped into two broader types: employee behaviours that are directed to individuals (OCB-I) and those that are directed to the organization (OCB-O) (McNeely and Meglino, 1994; Williams and Anderson, 1991).[1] Researchers have also explored a variety of predictors and outcomes that are related to citizenship behaviours (See Figure 1.1 for brief summary). In a broad sense, research has concluded that employee citizenship behaviours are important because they are likely to positively influence organizational effectiveness through their effects on how social systems within the organization work, how employees feel, and the effect that these behaviours have on task performance (Organ, 1997).

The second type of citizenship behaviour explored in the organizational literature has been *corporate citizenship*. Corporate citizenship is generally defined as the extent to which businesses engage in behaviours that will help them meet the economic, legal, ethical, and discretionary responsibilities imposed on them by their stakeholders (Maignan and Ferrell, 2000, p. 284). This concept is often connected to the idea that organizations have a degree of social responsibility to all their important stakeholders. Thus, some researchers refer to it as corporate social responsibility (CSR) or corporate ethics (Aguinis and Glavas, 2012; Carroll, 1998; Matten and Crane, 2005). There have been multiple conceptualizations of what counts as corporate citizenship. For example, Carroll (1998) suggests that there are four sides to corporate citizenship. The economic side encompasses the company's need to be profitable, reward their investors with a strong return on their investments, and assure other stakeholders of the continuity of the business so they can be "good corporate citizens". The legal side speaks of "good citizens" functioning in compliance with the law. A third side references the need for leaders and organizations to support and enact strong ethical values to be "good citizens" for society. This part is concerned with the ethical

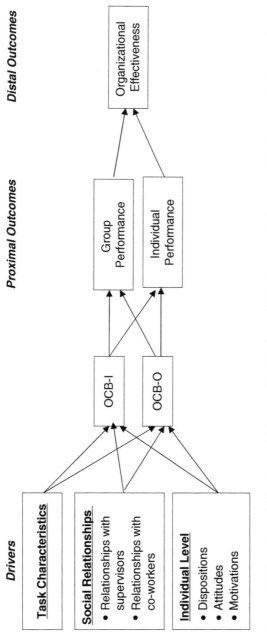

Figure 1.1 Overview of Nomological Network for Employee OCBs based on Spitzmuller, Van Dyne, and Ilies (2008).

12 Neus Feliu and Isabel C. Botero

responsibility of leaders and their fairness practices. Finally, the philanthropic side describes discretionary responsibilities which describe "corporate citizens" as those who strive to contribute resources to the community that they are part of.

Using a human resource perspective, Brammer, Millington and Rayton (2007) propose a different framework that suggests that corporate citizenship (i.e. which they label CSR) can be thought of as being focused inside and outside of the organization. Internal corporate citizenship behaviours are those that are performed by the organization that affect internal members (i.e. employees) and internal operations. These include behaviours such as employee training, continuous education, safe working environments, and ethical labour practices (Rupp and Mallory, 2015). External corporate citizenship is behaviours directed to external stakeholders and includes activities such as philanthropy, volunteering initiatives, community/economic development programs, and environmental sustainability programs (Rupp and Mallory, 2015).

The rise of research that focuses on corporate citizenship is linked to a growing pressure that stakeholders (i.e. customers, activists, governments, and media) place on companies to account for the social consequences of their activities, and the financial risks associated with conduct that is deemed unacceptable (Porter and Kramer, 2006). Research in corporate citizenship has tried to understand the drivers and outcomes associated with these behaviours. However, due to the relevance of corporate citizenship to the firm, most of the research has focused on understanding the effects of corporate citizenship on organizational performance (See: Aguinis and Glavas, 2012 for a detailed review) and on employee attitudes and behaviours (See: Aguinis and Glavas, 2012, and Podsakoff *et al.*, 2009 for detailed reviews). Figure 1.2 provides an overview of predictors and outcomes explored.

Even though corporate and employee citizenship behaviours have been studied separately, some scholars have tried to explore the connections between these two behaviours (See Aguinis and Glavas (2012) for a detailed review). For example, Lin *et al.* (2010) find that corporate citizenship behaviours (i.e. legal, and ethical citizenship) have a strong and significant influence on individual citizenship behaviours. That is, organizations that engage in corporate citizenship behaviours are likely to have employees who are more likely to engage in organizational citizenship behaviour. Thus, although these forms of citizenship are often seen as independent, they are likely to influence one another. This is important because it highlights two issues. First, although citizenship behaviours are often studied at one level of analysis, a wholistic understanding of these constructs requires the consideration of multiple levels of analysis. In addition, there is an interrelationship between the different levels of citizenship that will affect the behaviours at other levels. Therefore, to move forward in the field we need to understand

Citizenship Behaviours in Family Enterprises 13

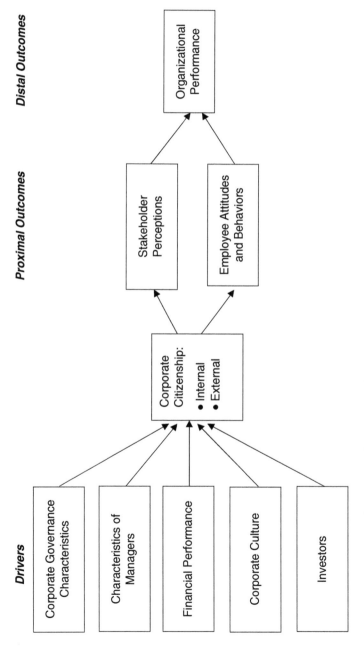

Figure 1.2 Overview of Drivers and Outcomes of Corporate Citizenship.

14 *Neus Feliu and Isabel C. Botero*

the multi-level dimensionality of citizenship behaviours and how these levels interact.

Citizenship Behaviours in the Family Enterprise

The overlap of family and business systems that can occur in the family enterprise[2] context provides an interesting setting to understand citizenship behaviours. Decision-making in these contexts is more complex because of the factors that are at play when making decisions (i.e. need to take into consideration both family and business goals) and the inherent consequences that organizational behaviours can have for the individual, the family, and the organization. This has led to the development of three broad lines of research that explore citizenship behaviours in family enterprises. The first line of research has focused on understanding the differences between family and non-family firms with regard to their corporate citizenship behaviours. Research in this area has found that family-controlled firms are more likely to consider the welfare of their stakeholders, which affects their citizenship behaviour (Craig and Dibrell, 2006; Dyer and Whetten, 2006). Researchers indicate that family businesses exhibit higher levels of corporate social responsibility and community citizenship in comparison to non-family firms (Berrone *et al.*, 2010; Craig and Dibrell, 2006; Dyer and Whetten, 2006; Kashmiri and Mahajan, 2010).

The second line of research has explored citizenship behaviours of family enterprises. This general work has tried to understand the extent to which different types of goals, the composition of the board, family business values, leadership beliefs, presence of family, family business culture, and stakeholder pressure influence whether family firms engage in corporate citizenship behaviours and how they do it. Findings from this work suggest that family firms are not homogeneous in how or why they engage in citizenship behaviours (Déniz Déniz and Suárez Cabrera, 2005). Interestingly, most of the research about corporate citizenship has centred on exploring the predictors of citizenship behaviour and not much has been explored regarding the outcomes associated with corporate CSR. Table 1.1 provides a summary of what has we know about this corporate citizenship in family firms.

The third line of research on citizenship behaviours in family enterprises has focused on employee citizenship behaviour. To our knowledge, there are only six papers that have been published in this area. These studies have found that psychological ownership, degree of identification with the family and the organization, organizational commitment, spiritual well-being, and supervisors' familial status are likely to influence the degree to which family and non-family employees engage in OCBs (Bernhard and O'Driscoll, 2011; Madison and Kellermanns, 2013; Matherne *et al.*, 2017; Marler and Stanley, 2018; McLarty *et al.*, 2019; Ramos *et al.*, 2014).

Table 1.1 Summary of Citizenship Research in Family Firms

Type of Citizenship	Type of Paper	Factors Studied/Proposed	Articles
Corporate	Conceptual	• Family-centred and Business centred goals as predictors of corporate citizenship in family enterprises.	Binz Astrachan *et al.* (2017) Cennamo *et al.*, (2012)
	Empirical	• Women presence in the board as predictor of citizenship behaviours of a firm. • SEW as predictors of corporate citizenship in family firms. • SEW goals as predictor corporate citizenship (i.e. environmentally responsible behaviour). • Role that family business values play in the extent to which a firm engages in CSR. • Percentage as equity as a predictor of corporate citizenship (i.e. CSR). • SEW dimensions as predictors of CSR engagement of family firms. • Pressure from Stakeholders and CSR-oriented leadership beliefs influence the implementation of CSR practices in Family Firms in India. • The presence of family in the management of the firm influences CSR Concerns in Family Firms • Family Firms with Family CEOs have better CSR performance • Family Business Culture affects Corporate Citizenship	Block and Wagner (2014) Campopiano *et al.*, (2019) Cruz *et al.*, (2014) Cui et al., (2018) Kim *et al.* (2019) Labelle *et al.* (2018) Marques *et al.*, (2014) Singh and Mittal (2019)
Employee OCB	Conceptual	• Identification & family friendship as predictors	Marler and Stanley (2018)
	Empirical	• Organizational and family identification as predictors of family and non-family employee OCB. • Psychological ownership as a predictor of family and non-family employee OCB. • Spiritual well-being as predictor of family and Non-family OCB • Organizational commitment, supervisor familial status, and the importance of SEW for supervisors as predictors of employee OCB.	Bernhard and O'Driscoll (2011) Madison and Kellermanns (2013) Matherne *et al.* (2017) McLarty *et al.*, (2019) Ramos *et al.* (2014)

16 *Neus Feliu and Isabel C. Botero*

Even though the seeds to our understanding about citizenship behaviours in family enterprises have been planted, one aspect that has not been considered is the role business families play in the citizenship behaviours of family enterprises. For example, Seaman (2017) argues that even though family enterprises are relevant economic actors worldwide and represent important pillars to the economies of most developed countries, the family has not yet been factored in when studying corporate citizenship in family enterprises. Binz Astrachan *et al.* (2017) supplement this idea by suggesting that the duality of goals family businesses pursue (i.e. family goals and business goals) are likely to affect whether these companies engage in citizenship behaviours and how they engage in them. Thus, to have a comprehensive understanding of citizenship behaviours in the family enterprise context, it is paramount to clarifying the role that the family system plays in these behaviours. We argue that one way of doing this is by taking a multilevel view of citizenship in the family enterprise. We discuss this idea in the next section.

Multi-level Nature of Citizenship Behaviours in Family Enterprises

When understanding citizenship behaviours, researchers have suggested that there are different types of behaviours that are included within citizenship. For example, Organ (1988) and Organ, Podsakoff and MacKenzie (2006) described Organizational Citizenship Behaviour (OCB) as encompassing five dimensions: (1) altruism (i.e. behaviour helps alleviate the work aimed at individuals in an organization), (2) courtesy (i.e. helping co-workers prevent problems related to their work by giving consultation and information and respecting their needs), (3) sportsmanship (i.e. having tolerance for situations that are not ideal at work without complaining), (4) civic virtue (i.e. extent to which employees are involved in organizational activities and care about the survival of the organization), and (5) conscientiousness (i.e. to do things that benefit the organization such as obeying the rules in the organization). Similarly, Van Dyne, Cummings and McLean Parks (1995) suggest that citizenship behaviours can be described as encompassing affiliative, challenging, promotive, and prohibitive behaviours. LePine, Erez and Johnson (2002) proposed an alternative model and suggest that at the employee level organizational citizenship behaviours include five dimensions: satisfaction, commitment, fairness, leader support, and conscientiousness. However, more recently, the exploration of dimensionality of citizenship behaviours has also included the idea of levels of analysis. For example, Aguinis and Glavas (2012) use levels of analysis as a way to better understand corporate social responsibility (i.e. corporate citizenship). They argue that citizenship behaviours (i.e. CSR) can be enacted at all levels of analysis (i.e. institutional, organizational, individual), and that it is important to understand how citizenship behaviours occur at different levels, and how the behaviour at these different levels of analysis can interact and influence one another.

We believe that taking a multilevel approach can also be very useful within the family business context because it can help acknowledge the different actors and systems that need to be considered to understand citizenship behaviours in this context. To us, citizenship behaviours in family firms are unique because they go beyond the consideration of individual and organizational behaviours to include the actions of the business-owning family. Family business scholars often indicate that behaviours of family firms are complex because of the interaction between the family and the business systems and the power that the family has, to affect the actions of the business (Chrisman *et al.*, 2012; Habbershon *et al.*, 2003; Kotlar and De Massis, 2013; Sharma, 2004). Thus, to understand the behaviours within the family business context it is important to explore the family system, its characteristics, and behaviours. We build on this idea to argue for a multilevel view of citizenship for family enterprises.

From our perspective, citizenship behaviours in family enterprises are enacted at three different levels: The individual, the family, and the enterprise/corporate level. Individual citizenship behaviours are consistent with what the organizational behaviour and management literature describe as organizational citizenship behaviours. These behaviours are discretionary in nature (i.e. a matter of personal choice), and, at the aggregate level promote the effective functioning of the organization (Organ, 1988). Family enterprise citizenship behaviours reflect the broader corporate citizenship behaviour literature and represent the actions and policies that organizations engage in to follow the expectations that stakeholders have regarding the triple bottom line (i.e. economic, social, and environmental performance; Aguinis, 2011). At the family level, we talk about business family citizenship behaviour. The following section introduces and defines this construct.

Business Family Citizenship Behaviour

Although business families play a central role in the direction of family enterprises, in the last two decades family business research has paid more attention to the business than the family side of the enterprise (Combs *et al.*, 2019). This omission has extended into the research about citizenship behaviours in family enterprises because there has not been a systematic consideration of the role that the family as a unit and system can affect these behaviours. As we mentioned earlier, the exploration of citizenship behaviours in family enterprises has only included citizenship behaviours of individual employees and the citizenship behaviours of the corporation. However, given that previous research supports the effect that the family system has on a range of firm behaviours such as altruism

18 *Neus Feliu and Isabel C. Botero*

(Schulze *et al.*, 2001), succession (Cabrera-Suárez *et al.*, 2001), governance (Anderson and Reeb, 2004), and corporate social responsibility (Dyer and Whetten, 2006), it is important to also understand how the family system influences other behaviours such as citizenship behaviours.

Family citizenship behaviours is a term used in the family science literature to describe a child's willingness to engage in behaviours that are both expected and go beyond role expectations and contribute to the family's overall functioning (Sibthorp *et al.*, 2013). However, the way that this construct has been previously defined describes actions at the individual level that have effects at the family level. This approach does not reflect the actions of the family unit. Thus, for this concept to be useful it requires a definition that acknowledges the group level nature of the construct (i.e. the family system). Using a group-level construct allows us to think about this construct differently, and it enables us to apply it to our multi-level framework. To do this we rely on previous work on citizenship behaviours at the team level.

Researchers argue that organizational citizenship behaviours at the team level are different from those at the individual level (Ehrhart and Naumann, 2004; Podsakoff *et al.*, 2014; Stoverink *et al.*, 2018). This has prompted a growing set of literature dedicated to explaining collective citizenship behaviours. Team level citizenship is different because it requires that members collectively behave in a similar way by integrating and coordinating their actions (Li *et al.*, 2014). For this to occur, the team needs to have descriptive norms (i.e. acceptance of team members that engaging in a certain behaviour is expected and accepted) that influence the behaviours of all members. Therefore, team level citizenship behaviours should represent more than the addition of all individual actions to a team level, they should reflect the behaviours of the team as a whole and should benefit both the team and the organization (Podsakoff *et al.*, 2014). We build on these ideas to define the business family citizenship behaviour construct.

Business family citizenship behaviours (BFCB) are behaviours and policies of business family units that contribute to the maintenance and enhancement of the social and psychological context that supports the overall functioning of the family unit and the family enterprise. Multiple behaviours can be encompassed within this type of citizenship behaviour. However, two dimensions that are useful to describe these behaviours are: (1) to whom the behaviour is directed? And (2) what is the purpose of the behaviour? Implied in our definition of BFCB is the idea that these behaviours can be directed at the family or at the family enterprise (i.e. business). Thus, we can use this idea as our first dimension in that BFCB can be directed at helping the family or at helping the family enterprise. To explain the second dimension, we build on the work of Van Dyne, Cummings and McLean Parks (1995) who suggest that citizenship behaviours can have an affiliative (i.e. to strengthen relationships) or challenging (i.e. to challenge the current status quo) purpose. Based on these arguments, we believe that there are four types of BFCB that are relevant in the family enterprise. The first group of BFCB are those that are directed at the family with the purpose of strengthening the relationship between family members. These behaviours help reduce relational conflict in the family, enhance the behaviours of the family as a cohesive unit, and help develop dynamics that create healthy relationships between family members. The second group of BFCB are those directed at the family but that is challenging in nature. Challenging citizenship behaviours are those that question the current state of the family. For example, when a family has an internal conflict or people who are not respecting family rules, members engage in BFCB by explicitly acknowledging the inconsistent actions of others and explaining how they are hurting the family or the business. By doing this, they bring awareness to the issue, or enable the issue to be discussed by the different family members. The third group of BFCB are those that are directed at the family enterprise with the purpose of strengthening the relationship between the business-owning family and the family enterprise. An example of these actions can be the development of training programs regarding how to become responsible owners of the firm. When a family creates these sorts of programs, they are able to strengthen the relationship of the family unit to the business. The fourth and final group of BFCB are those directed at the family enterprise and that are challenging the current state of the business. Examples of these behaviours can include making constructive suggestions of how to improve the relationship between the family and the business, explaining how to improve business processes to benefit the family enterprise. Combined these four types of behaviours will reflect the actions of the family that can influence both the family and the business. Table 1.2 provides definitions and examples of the four-business family citizenship behaviours.

To fully understand the citizenship behaviours of a business family we need to understand what factors drive this behaviour, and the outcomes that are associated with the behaviour. The following two sections present the drivers and outcomes based on the literature on organizational citizenship behaviours, family business literature, and our work with enterprising families.

Drivers of Business Family Citizenship Behaviours

To fully understand the citizenship behaviours of a business family we also need to understand what are the different factors that will drive the family's collective citizenship behaviour. There are at least three sets of predictors that need to be considered to understand the business family citizenship behaviour. These are: (1) the individual characteristics of

20   *Neus Feliu and Isabel C. Botero*

Table 1.2 Types of Business Family Citizenship Behaviors

	Directed at the Business Family	*Directed at the Family Enterprise*
Affiliative Behaviors	These citizenship behaviours and policies focus on strengthening the relationships between the members of business-owning families. Examples include: • Being informed and educated on family matters. • Making efforts to be an active member of the family by participating in family activities.	These citizenship behaviours and policies focus on strengthening the relationships between the members of business-owning families and their family enterprises. Examples include: • Being active and responsible owners • Becoming informed and educated on family enterprise matters. • Becoming a steward of the business.
Challenging Behaviors	These citizenship behaviours and policies focus on challenging the status quo of the family with the intent of helping. Examples include: • Engaging in constructive criticism regarding family dynamics or family interactions. • Challenging individuals to become better family members or family stewards.	These citizenship behaviours and policies focus on challenging the current status quo to improve the family enterprise. Examples include: • Making constructive suggestions of how to improve the relationship between the family and the business. • Voicing ideas of how to improve the business.

family members, (2) the characteristics of family leaders, and (3) the characteristics of the family context.

Previous research in the organizational citizenship behaviour area argues that individual characteristics of members are important to consider when exploring group level citizenship behaviours. For example, LePine and Van Dyne (1998) find that self-esteem and satisfaction with the group are important at predicting voice behaviours (i.e. a type of individual citizenship behaviour). Podsakoff *et al.* (2000) complement this understanding by outlining the different individual-level antecedents of citizenship behaviours (i.e. attitudes, dispositional variables, individual perceptions, and demographic variables). The meta-analysis by Chiaburu *et al.* (2011) complements this by showing how the five-factor model of personality acts as a predictor of aggregate citizenship behaviours. Thus, there is ample evidence that individual-level factors matter

Citizenship Behaviours in Family Enterprises 21

in determining whether there are unit-level citizenship behaviours. When considering business family citizenship behaviours, we argue that there are at least three individual-level factors that need to be considered as predictors of the family level citizenship behaviour. The first personal driver is the individual's motivation to engage with the family. For the family to act as a unified unit, members of the family need to be willing to engage with one another. For example, individuals who are willing to engage with the family will also be inclined to actively learn about the business family and the family enterprise so they can understand the role of the family and its responsibilities towards the business. The second personal driver is the time commitment to the family (i.e. the willingness to devote time to the family and participate as part of the family in its activities). Given the multiple responsibilities and commitments of individual's today, individuals need to show commitment to the family so they can be active members of the business family and be willing to dedicate time to helping the family and the business be better. The final driver is the individual's personal goals, and the place that the family has in those goals. When individuals have goals that incorporate the family, they will be more likely to want to engage with their family unit and engage in behaviours as a unit.

The second set of drivers for business family citizenship behaviours is related to the characteristics of the family business leaders and the types of relationships that they develop with other family members. Previous research in organizational citizenship behaviour provides ample evidence of the role that leaders play in facilitating employee citizenship behaviours. For example, Pearce and Herbik (2004) also found that the extent to which leaders encouraged teamwork increased team citizenship behaviours. White and Lean (2008) leader integrity is likely to influence the citizenship and ethical behaviours of employees. Furthermore, a meta-analysis by Ilies, Nahrgang and Morgeson (2007) suggests that the actions of leaders are likely to have a strong influence on individual-oriented citizenship behaviours. Thus, it is important to consider the behaviour of leaders as a driver of business family citizenship behaviour. From our perspective, family leaders play an important role in teaching and motivating family members to become part of and act as a family unit. Thus, when family leaders are controlling and do not promote family participation and interaction, the probabilities that a family unit will engage in citizenship behaviours as a group will diminish. However, when family leaders promote family interaction and facilitate learning within the family, this will result in higher likelihood that the family will want to act as a unit in their citizenship behaviour.

The third set of drivers that are important to consider is those at the family level. Research in the organizational citizenship behaviour literature suggests that the characteristics of the team (i.e. size, cohesion, formalization of the structure, team climate) are likely to influence

22 Neus Feliu and Isabel C. Botero

whether or not individuals engage in citizenship behaviour (Lin *et al.*, 2010; Podsakoff *et al.*, 2000). Similarly, the characteristics of the family unit are likely to affect the actions of families (Björnberg and Nicholson, 2007; Déniz Déniz and Suárez Cabrera, 2005: Marques *et al.*, 2014; Sorenson and Bierman, 2009). Thus, we argue that there are at least four family characteristics that can drive the likelihood of a family engaging in citizenship behaviours as a unit. The first factor is how the family defines its boundaries. This determines who is included in the activities of the family and who is excluded from the activities of the family. We believe that higher levels of inclusivity will enhance the likelihood of family members willing to be active within the family. We believe that the inclusion of in-laws for example is likely to increase the willingness of their spousal family members to interact with the family. At the same time, the greater the number of people included as part of the family, the more difficult it is to get all members to act as one unit. The second family drivers are related to family values: the types of values that the family holds, and how shared these values are. Previous literature indicates the importance of family values in the family business (Chrisman *et al.*, 2012; Marques *et al.*, 2014; Sundaramurthy and Kreiner, 2008). Thus, we believe that families who share self-transcendent values (i.e. those that emphasize concern for the welfare and interests of others; also known as collective values; Schwartz, 1992; Stern and Dietz, 1994; Stern, Dietz, and Guagnano, 1998) are more likely to be willing to engage in citizenship behaviours as a unit. The third driver is the goals of the business family. The goals of family businesses are dual in nature. They include both financial and non-financial components (Dyer and Whetten, 2006; Gómez-Mejía et al., 2007). Thus, when business families share family and business centred goals this translates into greater care for non-family employees, suppliers, customers and the community at large (Miller and Le Breton-Miller, 2005); all of which are aspects of corporate citizenship behaviour. The last predictor at the family level is family cohesion. Olson (2000) defines family cohesion as the emotional bonding that family members have towards one another. We believe that the stronger the family cohesion the more the family is willing to work together. Figure 1.3 summarizes the drivers and outcomes associated with business family citizenship behaviour.

Outcomes Related to Business Family Citizenship Behaviours

One of the main reasons that we study citizenship behaviours in organizational contexts is because we are interested in the consequences of these behaviours (Podsakoff *et al.*, 2009). Citizenship behaviours are expected to have positive consequences for the organization, the group and the individual. Thus, introducing the business family citizenship

Citizenship Behaviours in Family Enterprises 23

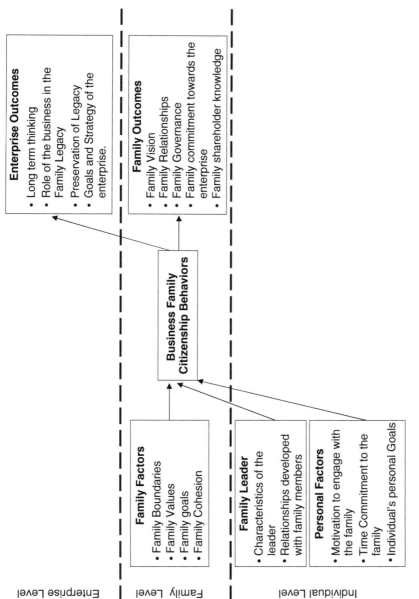

Figure 1.3 Business/Enterprising Family Citizenship.

behaviour construct, it is important to outline the outcomes that we expect it to influence. As explained earlier, we view these unit-level citizenship behaviours as influencing both the family and the business. Thus, we want to highlight some of the family and business outcomes that we expect it to influence. As we will develop in the last section of the chapter, we expect family and business outcomes to influence one another. However, we outline these independently.

There are five family outcomes that will be influenced by business family citizenship behaviours. The first is the vision of the family. Practising citizenship behaviours as a family will help families understand what they want for the future. For example, working together as a family can help families understand the purpose of their wealth and how they want to use it for the next generations. It may also help the family understand how they want to continue to generate wealth, what type of relationship the family wants to have with the enterprise, and how the family can engage or interact with the enterprise. A second outcome in the family that will be affected by engaging in citizenship behaviours as a family is relationships between family members. We suggest that business family citizenship behaviours enhance the bonding between family members, their interaction patterns, their involvement in family matters, and strengths of ties among relatives. This, in turn, translates into higher levels of family trust. Trust represents a key relational issue in family enterprises, and it is fundamental for cooperation, information flow, and knowledge sharing. It also helps create unique capabilities for the family enterprise (Pearson and Carr, 2011). Family governance is another factor that is affected by the citizenship behaviours of the family. We believe that enterprising families that have strong family citizenship invest in defining and developing governance structures that help them achieve their family and business goals. For example, engaging as a family in citizenship behaviours can affect how the family thinks about where the family's voice will reside in the chosen structure, or how to best incorporate independent expertise. They will also be able to understand and develop opportunities for involvement of family members who want to play an active role in management or an advisory role in one of the areas of the family enterprise (e.g. family governance, investment committee, philanthropic or impact investing committee).

Working as a family unit will also affect the family shareholder knowledge. Engaging in citizenship behaviours as a family, allows all members to understand what the business contributes to the family and how this contribution occurs. Thus, it helps develop an understanding of ownership, which can influence interest in the responsibilities of shareholders. Recent work by Astrachan *et al.* (2020) highlights the importance of creating opportunities to educate family members about committed and sustainable ownership, which can be one of the outcomes of working together as a family. Finally, business family citizenship behaviour is also likely to result in higher commitment to family-centred goals (i.e. the common mindset among family members in terms of their feelings of loyalty to the family and the desire to invest mental and physical energy in helping to achieve family-centred goals; Kotlar and De Massis, 2013). Family member commitment their willingness to go beyond their role to help the family business (Sharma and Irving, 2005).

Implied in our definition of business family citizenship behaviour is the belief that one of the reasons why these behaviours are important is because they will help support the overall family enterprise. Therefore, we believe that these actions will affect the family enterprise in several ways. Engaging in citizenship behaviours as a family should affect the desire of the family to support the continuity of the family enterprise. In particular, citizenship behaviour of the business family is likely the long-term thinking capability of family members, which will impact the willingness of the family to be engaged with the business, and the willingness to continue in the enterprising journey. A second factor that is influenced by the citizenship behaviours of the family is a deep understanding of the role the business plays in the family legacy. When families engage in citizenship behaviours together they are able to understand where they come from and where they want to go in the future. Having a clear understanding of the legacy helps the family understand the importance that the enterprise plays in that legacy. This, in turn, helps family members develop a sense of responsibility for the preservation of that legacy and one way to do this is through stewardship behaviours. Thus, helping family members understand their legacy will impact how the business family relates to the family enterprise, and the responsibility that they feel when they are part of the management and ownership of the firm. Family business citizenship behaviours also play a role in how the family thinks about the goals and strategy of the family enterprise. The family business literature supports the importance of families perceiving their business as relevant. When businesses are relevant to families, the family influences the way that the business behaves, and the goals they pursue (Chrisman *et al.*, 2012). When families engage in citizenship behaviours together the connection between family members and the business strengthens through the shared experiences of family members from different generations.

Now that we have a general understanding of the family level citizenship behaviours within family enterprises, we now turn to understand the interconnectivity between the different levels of citizenship.

Interconnections Between Citizenship Behaviours at Multiple Levels of Analysis

Research about citizenship behaviours in organizations supports the strong interconnection between organizational and individual citizenship behaviours (Aguinis and Glavas, 2012; Lin *et al.*, 2010). We build on two theories to further explain why citizenship behaviours at different levels of analysis are likely to influence one another. Social learning theory is a framework used to explain how individuals learn (Bandura, 1986). This theory argues that the way that we learn is by observing the behaviour of others. We observe others to understand how they do things, and the rewards and punishments that they receive for their actions. In organizations, we look at our co-workers to learn what we need to do to complete a job, and to understand which behaviours are appropriate and inappropriate (Woods and Bandura, 1989). When applied to help us understand citizenship behaviours in family enterprises this suggests that the more citizenship behaviours that are modelled/ performed by the owning family, the more likely the enterprise is to behave in similar ways. Similarly, the more the owning family engages in citizenship behaviours, the higher the possibility that employees for the family enterprise will behave in ways that are consistent with the family. This is particularly true when there is a high overlap between the identities of the family and the business (Sundaramurthy and Kreiner, 2008) and when the behaviour is associated with positive consequences (Podsakoff and MacKenzie, 1997).

Social information processing theory (Salancik and Pfeffer, 1978) also support the interrelationship between the different levels of analysis of citizenship behaviour in family enterprises. This theoretical approach indicates that individuals are adaptive organisms that adapt their attitudes, behaviours and beliefs to their social context, and their reality. Thus, as individuals, we learn what behaviour we should follow by observing informational and social cues of the context where behaviour occurs. In other words, when we are part of an organization, a family, or an industry we are going to look at our immediate environment to determine the acceptability of citizenship behaviours. When citizenship behaviours are high among the family, the business, or other employees, we are going to interpret this as a cue that these behaviours are acceptable and expected within the context. This suggests that if I am an employee in a family enterprise and see the business family that is highly connected to the business, then I am going to perceive that citizenship behaviours are expected within the context. We see these ideas applying when examining the different interconnections between the individual, family and enterprise levels of analysis.

An important point that we want to highlight is that we see business family citizenship behaviour as the primary reference point for the individual and for the enterprise level. Even though family firms are heterogeneous (Déniz Déniz and Suárez Cabrera, 2005; Marques *et al.*, 2014), previous research analysing citizenship behaviours in family enterprises supports the central role that the family plays in these behaviours (Binz Astrachan *et al.*, 2017; Cennamo *et al.*, 2012;

Seaman, 2017). Thus, business family citizenship will influence both the enterprise and employee citizenship behaviours.

Conclusions and Directions for Future Research

This chapter explores the nature of citizenship in the family enterprise context. To achieve this goal, we focus on four issues. First, we define the concept of citizenship and summarize what we know about citizenship behaviours in family enterprises. We then propose a multi-level model to acknowledge the different systems that are at play when studying citizenship in family enterprises. This model suggests that within family enterprises the exploration of citizenship needs to acknowledge the individual, family, and enterprise level. Given that the family system has not been considered when exploring citizenship behaviours in family firms, we then introduce business family citizenship as a new construct. Building on the central role that the family system plays in the family enterprise, we argue that business family citizenship is a central idea to advance our of this area and field because behaviour at this level of analysis is likely to influence similar behaviours at the individual and enterprise levels of analysis.

Family Citizenship considers the impact and the value that a family adds to the enterprise from a broader perspective, that goes beyond the family's participation in management. We believe that it is important that as practitioners and as researchers we move beyond thinking that the only, or the more relevant way, in which family adds value to the business is through management. In the model, we propose the important role that the family can play as a unit. Based on this idea, we suggest that the first step for future research is to explore the citizenship behaviours of the family unit. This can be done through a qualitative approach (i.e. observation of families, interviews, or the use of archival data). Although we have observed this behaviour in practice, there is no systematic observation of families and the citizenship behaviours as a unit. Thus, it would be a good place to start. Another aspect that can be explored is whether the citizenship behaviours of the enterprise or the individual's (i.e. family and non-family employees) within the enterprise are affected by the citizenship actions of the family unit. Sundaramurthy and Kreiner (2008) argue that family enterprises differ in the degree to which the family and business identities overlap. Thus, we can build on this idea to explore under which conditions the citizenship behaviours of the family are connected to the behaviours of the business and when they are not. This could also help us understand whether the three levels of citizenship behaviour are connected or disconnected within the family firm. Finally, another avenue for future research is to explore the drivers and outcomes of citizenship behaviours at the different levels of analysis. This could help us better understand how the predictors and outcomes of

28 Neus Feliu and Isabel C. Botero

these behaviours are similar and different. In conclusion, we hope that this chapter helps us create new interest in research about citizenship behaviours within the family Enterprise.

Notes

1 Van Dyne, Cummings and McLean Parks (1995) also indicate that employee OCBs can be described as affiliative behaviours (i.e. those that strengthen relationships) and challenging (i.e., those that try to modify the status quo).
2 Although there are multiple definitions of what constitutes a family enterprise, we build on the Seaman (2017) and define family enterprises as organization(s) where a family controls one or more businesses and where the values of that family contribute to behaviour within those businesses, and hence to corporate citizenship.

References

Aguinis, H. (2011) 'Organizational responsibility: Doing good and doing well', in Zedeck S. (ed.), *APA handbook of industrial and organizational psychology*. Washington, DC: American Psychological Association, Vol. 3, pp. 855–879.

Aguinis, H. and Glavas, A. (2012) 'What we know and don't know about corporate social responsibility: A review and research agenda', *Journal of Management*, 38(4), pp. 932–968.

Anderson, R.C. and Reeb, D.M. (2004) 'Board composition: Balancing family influence in S&P 500 firms', *Administrative Science Quarterly*, 49, pp. 209–237.

Astrachan, C. *et al.* (2020) 'Professionalizing the business family: The five pillars of competent, committed, and sustainable ownership', *Research Report for the 2086 Society & Family Firm Institute*. Available at https://digital. ffi. org/pdf/ wednesday-edition/2020/january-08/ffi_professionalizing_the_business_family_v2. Pdf

Bandura, A. (1986) *Social foundations of thought and action*. NJ: Englewood Cliffs.

Barnard, C. (1938) *The functions of the executive*. Cambridge, MA: Harvard University Press.

Barnett, M.L. and Salomon, R.M. (2012) 'Does it pay to be really good? Addressing the shape of the relationship between social and financial performance', *Strategic Management Journal*, 33(11), pp. 1304–1320.

Bernhard, F. and O'Driscoll, M.P. (2011) 'Psychological ownership in small family-owned businesses: Leadership style and nonfamily-employees' work attitudes and behaviors', *Group & Organization Management*, 36(3), pp. 345–384.

Berrone, P. *et al.* (2010) 'Socioemotional wealth and corporate responses to institutional pressures: Do family-controlled firms pollute less?' *Administrative Science Quarterly*, 55(1), pp. 82–113.

Binz Astrachan, C. *et al.* (2017) 'Family business goals, corporate citizenship behaviour and firm performance: Disentangling the connections', *International Journal of Management and Enterprise Development*, 16(1–2), pp. 34–56.

Björnberg, Å. and Nicholson, N. (2007) 'The family climate scales—Development of a new measure for use in family business research', *Family Business Review*, 20(3), pp. 229–246.

Block, J. and Wagner, M. (2014) 'Ownership versus management effects on corporate social responsibility concerns in large family and founder firms', *Journal of Family Business Strategy*, 5(4), pp. 339–346.

Brammer, S., Millington, A. and Rayton, B. (2007) 'The contribution of corporate social responsibility to organizational commitment', *International Journal Human Resource Management*, 18, pp. 1701–1719.

Cabrera-Suárez, K., De Saá-Pérez, P. and Garcia-Almeida, D. (2001) 'The succession process from a resource- and knowledge-based view of the family firm', *Family Business Review*, 14, pp. 37–46.

Campopiano, G. *et al.* (2019) 'Family and non-family women on the board of directors: Effects on corporate citizenship behavior in family-controlled fashion firms', *Journal of Cleaner Production*, 214, pp. 41–51.

Carroll, A.B. (1979) 'A three-dimensional conceptual model of corporate performance', *Academy of Management Review*, 4(4), pp. 497–505.

Carroll, A.B. (1998) 'The four faces of corporate citizenship', *Business and Society Review*, 100–101(1), pp. 1–7.

Cennamo, C. *et al.* (2012) 'Socioemotional wealth and proactive stakeholder engagement: Why family – controlled firms care more about their stakeholder's entrepreneurship', *Theory and Practice*, 36, pp. 1153–1173.

Chiaburu, D.S. *et al.* (2011) 'The five-factor model of personality traits and organizational citizenship behaviors: A meta-analysis', *Journal of Applied Psychology*, 96(6), pp. 1140.

Chrisman, J.J. *et al.* (2012) 'Family involvement, family influence, and family-centered non-economic goals in small firms', *Entrepreneurship Theory and Practice*, 36(2), pp. 267–293.

Craig, J. and Dibrell, C. (2006) 'The natural environment, innovation, and firm performance: A comparative study', *Family Business Review*, 19, pp. 275–288.

Cruz, C. *et al.* (2014) 'Are family firms really more socially responsible?' *Entrepreneurship Theory and Practice*, 38(6), pp. 1295–1316.

Combs, J.G. *et al.* (2019) 'What do we know about business families? Setting the stage for leveraging family science theories', *Family Business Review*, 38(1), pp. 38–63, 0894486519863508.

Cui, V. *et al.* (2018) 'Revisiting the effect of family involvement on corporate social responsibility: A behavioral agency perspective', *Journal of Business Ethics*, 152(1), pp. 291–309.

Déniz Déniz, M.D.L. and Suárez Cabrera, M.K. (2005) 'Corporate social responsibility and family business in Spain', *Journal of Business Ethics*, 56(1), pp. 27–41.

Dyer Jr W.G. and Whetten, D.A. (2006) 'Family firms and social responsibility: Preliminary evidence from the S&P 500', *Entrepreneurship Theory and Practice*, 30(6), pp. 785–802.

Ehrhart, M.G. and Naumann, S.E. (2004) 'Organizational citizenship behavior in work groups: A group norms approach', *Journal of Applied Psychology*, 89(6), pp. 960.

30 *Neus Feliu and Isabel C. Botero*

Godfrey, P.C. (2005) 'The relationship between corporate philanthropy and shareholder wealth: A risk management perspective', *Academy of Management Review*, 30 (49), pp. 777–798.

Gómez-Mejía, L.R. *et al.* (2007) 'Socioemotional wealth and business risks in family-controlled firms: Evidence from Spanish olive oil mills', *Administrative Science Quarterly*, 52(1), pp. 106–137.

Graham, J.W. (1986) 'Principled organizational dissent: A theoretical essay', in Staw B.M. and Cummings L.L. (eds.), *Research in organizational behavior*. Greenwich CT: JAI Press, Vol 8, pp. 1–50.

Graham, J.W. (1991) 'An essay on organizational citizenship behavior', *Employee Responsibilities and Rights Journal*, 4(4), pp. 249–270.

Graham, J.W. (2000) 'Promoting civic virtue organizational citizenship behavior: Contemporary questions rooted in classical quandaries from political philosophy', *Human Resource Management Review*, 10(1), pp. 61–77.

Habbershon, T.G., Williams, M., and MacMillan, I.C. (2003) 'A unified systems perspective of family firm performance', *Journal of Business Venturing*, 18(4), pp. 451–465.

Ilies, R., Nahrgang, J.D. and Morgeson, F.P. (2007) 'Leader-member exchange and citizenship behaviors: A meta-analysis', *Journal of Applied Psychology*, 92(1), pp. 269.

Katz, D. (1964) 'The motivational basis of organizational behavior', *Behavioral Science*, 9, pp. 131–146.

Kashmiri, S., and Mahajan, V. (2010) 'What's in a name?: An analysis of the strategic behavior of family firms', *International Journal of Research in Marketing*, 27(3), pp. 271–280.

Kim, K. *et al.* (2019) 'Corporate social performance of family firms: A place-based perspective in the context of layoffs', *Journal of Business Ethics*, 167, pp. 1–18.

Kotlar, J. and De Massis, A. (2013) 'Goal setting in family firms: Goal diversity, social interactions, and collective commitment to family–centered goals', *Entrepreneurship Theory and Practice*, 37(6), pp. 1263–1288.

Labelle, R. *et al.* (2018) 'Family firms' corporate social performance: A calculated quest for socioemotional wealth', *Journal of Business Ethics*, 148(3), pp. 511–525.

LePine, J.A., Erez, A. and Johnson, D.E. (2002) 'The nature and dimensionality of organizational citizenship behavior: a critical review and meta-analysis', *Journal of Applied Psychology*, 87(1), pp. 52.

LePine, J.A. and Van Dyne, L. (1998) 'Predicting voice behavior in work groups', *Journal of Applied Psychology*, 83(6), pp. 853.

Li, N., Chiaburu, D.S. and Kirkman, B.L. (2017) 'Cross-level influences of empowering leadership on citizenship behavior: Organizational support climate as a double-edged sword', *Journal of Management*, 43(4), pp. 1076–1102.

Li, N., Kirkman, B.L. and Porter, C.O. (2014) 'Toward a model of work team altruism', *Academy of Management Review*, 39(4), pp. 541–565.

Lin, C.P. *et al.* (2010) 'Modeling corporate citizenship and its relationship with organizational citizenship behaviors', *Journal of Business Ethics*, 95(3), pp. 357–372.

Madison, K. and Kellermanns, F.W. (2013) 'Is the spiritual bond bound by blood? An exploratory study of spiritual leadership in family firms', *Journal of Management, Spirituality & Religion*, 10(2), pp. 159–182.

Maignan, I. and Ferrell, O.C. (2000) 'Measuring corporate citizenship in two countries: The case of the United States and France', *Journal of Business Ethics*, 23(3), pp. 283–297.

Marler, L.E. and Stanley, L.J. (2018) 'Commentary: Who are your friends? The influence of identification and family in-group and out-group friendships on nonfamily employee OCB and deviance', *Entrepreneurship Theory and Practice*, 42(2), pp. 310–316.

Marques, P., Presas, P. and Simon, A. (2014) 'The heterogeneity of family firms in CSR engagement: The role of values', *Family Business Review*, 27(3), pp. 206–227.

Matherne, C. *et al.* (2017) 'Beyond organizational identification: The legitimization and robustness of family identification in the family firm', *Journal of Family Business Strategy*, 8(3), pp. 170–184.

Matten, D. and Crane, A. (2005) 'Corporate citizenship: Toward an extended theoretical conceptualizatio', *Academy of Management review*, 30(1), pp. 166–179.

McLarty, B.D., Vardaman, J.M. and Barnett, T. (2019) 'Congruence in exchange: The influence of supervisors on employee performance in family firms', *Entrepreneurship Theory and Practice*, 43(2), pp. 302–321.

McNeely, B.L. and Meglino, B.M. (1994) 'The role of dispositional and situational antecedents in prosocial organizational behavior: An examination of the intended beneficiaries of prosocial behavior', *Journal of Applied Psychology*, 79(6), pp. 836.

Miller, D. and Le Breton-Miller, I. (2005) *Managing for the long run: Lessons in competitive advantage from great family businesses*. Harvard Business Press.

Miller, D., Le Breton-Miller, I. and Scholnick, B. (2008) 'Stewardship vs. stagnation: An empirical comparison of small family and non-family businesses', *Journal of Management Studies*, 45(1), pp. 51–78.

Olson, D.H. (2000) 'Circumplex model of marital and family systems', *Journal of family Therapy*, 22(2), pp. 144–167.

Organ, D.W. (1988) *Organizational citizenship behavior: The good soldier syndrome*. Lexington, MA: Lexington Books.

Organ, D.W. (1997) 'Organizational citizenship behavior: It's construct clean-up time', *Human performance*, 10(2), pp. 85–97.

Organ, D.W., Podsakoff, P.M. and MacKenzie, S.B. (2006) *Organizational citizenship behavior: Its nature, antecedents, and consequences*. Sage Publications.

Pearce, C.L. and Herbik, P.A. (2004) 'Citizenship behavior at the team level of analysis: The effects of team leadership, team commitment, perceived team support, and team size', *The Journal of Social Psychology*, 144(3), pp. 293–310.

Podsakoff, P.M. and MacKenzie, S.B. (1997) 'Impact of organizational citizenship behavior on organizational performance: A review and suggestion for future research', *Human Performance*, 10(2), pp. 133–151.

Podsakoff, P.M. *et al.* (2000) Organizational citizenship behaviors: A critical review of the theoretical and empirical literature and suggestions for future research. *Journal of Management*, 26(3), pp. 513–563.

Podsakoff, N.P., *et al.* (2014) 'Consequences of unit-level organizational citizenship behaviors: A review and recommendations for future research', *Journal of Organizational Behavior*, 35(S1), pp. S87–S119.

Podsakoff, N.P. *et al.* (2009) 'Individual-and organizational-level consequences of organizational citizenship behaviors: A meta-analysis', *Journal of Applied Psychology*, 94(1), pp. 122.

Porter, M.E. and Kramer, M.R. (2006) *Strategy and society: The link between competitive advantage and corporate social responsibility*. Harvard Business Review.

Ramos, H.M. *et al.* (2014) 'Psychological ownership in small family firms: Family and non-family employees' work attitudes and behaviours', *Journal of Family Business Strategy*, 5(3), pp. 300–311.

Rupp, D.E. and Mallory, D.B. (2015) 'Corporate social responsibility: Psychological, person-centric, and progressing', *Annual Review of Organizational Psychology and Organizational Behavior*, 2(1), pp. 211–236.

Salancik, G.R. and Pfeffer, J. (1978) 'A social information processing approach to job attitudes and task design', *Administrative science quarterly*, 23(2), pp. 224–253.

Schulze, W.S. *et al.* (2001) 'Agency relationships in family firms: Theory and evidence', *Organization Science*, 12, pp. 99–116.

Schwartz, S.H. (1992) 'Universals in the content of and structure of values: Theoretical advances and empirical tests in 20 countries', *Advances in Experimental Social Psychology*, 25, pp. 1–65.

Seaman, C. (2017) 'Factoring the family into corporate citizenship', *The Journal of Corporate Citizenship*, 65, pp. 6–11.

Sharma, P. (2004) 'An overview of the field of family business studies: Current status and directions for the future', *Family Business Review*, 1, pp. 1–36.

Sharma, P. and Irving, P.G. (2005) 'Four bases of family business successor commitment: Antecedents and consequences', *Entrepreneurship Theory and Practice*, 29(1), pp. 13–33.

Sibthorp, J. *et al.* (2013) 'Validating, norming, and utility of a youth outcomes battery for recreation programs and camps', *Journal of Leisure Research*, 45(4), pp. 514–536.

Singh, S. and Mittal, S. (2019) 'Analysis of drivers of CSR practices' implementation among family firms in India: A stakeholder's perspective', *International Journal of Organizational Analysis*.

Sorenson, R.L. and Bierman, L. (2009) 'Family capital, family business, and free enterprise', *Family Business Review*, 22(3), pp. 193–195.

Spitzmuller, M., Van Dyne, L. and Ilies, R. (2008) 'Organizational citizenship behavior: A review and extension of its nomological network', *The SAGE handbook of organizational behavior*. New York: Sage, Vol. 1, pp. 106–123.

Stern, P.C. and Dietz, T. (1994) 'The value basis of environmental concern', *Journal of Social Issues*, 50, pp. 65–84.

Stern, P.C., Dietz, T. and Guagnano, G.A. (1998) 'A brief inventory of values', *Educational and Psychological Measurement*, 58, pp. 984–1001.

Stoverink, A.C. *et al.* (2018) 'Supporting team citizenship: The influence of team social resources on team-level affiliation-oriented and challenge-oriented behaviour', *Human Resource Management Journal*, 28(2), pp. 201–215.

Sundaramurthy, C. and Kreiner, G.E. (2008) 'Governing by managing identity boundaries: The case of family businesses', *Entrepreneurship Theory and Practice*, 32(3), pp. 415–436.

Van Dyne, L., Cummings, L.L. and McLean Parks, J. (1995) 'Extra-role behaviors: In pursuit of construct and definitional clarity (A bridge over muddied waters)', in Staw B. (ed.), *Research in organizational behavior*. London: Elsevier, Vol. 17, pp. 215–285.

Ward, J.L. (1997) 'Growing the family business: special challenges and best practices', *Family Business Review*, 10(4), pp. 323–337.

White, D.W. and Lean, E. (2008) 'The impact of perceived leader integrity on subordinates in a work team environment', *Journal of Business Ethics*, 81(4), pp. 765–778.

Williams, L.J. and Anderson, S.E. (1991) 'Job satisfaction and organizational commitment as predictors of organizational citizenship and in-role behaviors', *Journal of management*, 17(3), pp. 601–617.

Wood, R. and Bandura, A. (1989) 'Social cognitive theory of organizational management', *Academy of Management Review*, 14(3), pp. 361–384.

Zachary, R.K. (2011) 'The importance of the family system in family business', *Journal of Family Business Management*, 1(1), pp. 26–36.

2 Sustainability in Historic Family Firms

Anne Barraquier

Introduction

Some businesses have been around for a long time. These old business firms have endured numerous crises, attacks, and difficulties. They also have thrived to meet success and recognition. Amid these old firms, many are family-run businesses. These families have worked to make the family business flourish, passing it successfully from one generation to another (Korainen, 2002). Two issues have dominated research on family-owned businesses. One is whether they perform better economically than non-family owned. This issue has generated an enormous interest among management scholars (see Anderson and Reeb, 2003). Another issue is more contemporary. It questions the social and environmental performance of these firms (Dyer and Whetten, 2006). Given the positive correlation revealed by several studies (Berrone *et al.*, 2010), research efforts now tend to focus more on the underlying dynamics of this performance. Recent research has investigated behaviour, values and identity as antecedents of responsible behaviour in family firms, in the perspective of understanding the role of these determinants in corporate social responsibility (CSR).

This chapter presents a qualitative study conducted in the historic flavour and fragrance industry in the south of France. It investigates how explicit and tacit values are internally shared to eventually connect to CSR and sustainability commitment. The French Riviera is known for its beautiful sceneries and coastline, but one of its most valuable treasures lies in the ancestral know-how of perfume manufacturing. As early as the 16th century, the French nobility looked for fragrant materials to mask the unpleasant smell of leather gloves. It marked the beginning of the perfume industry for farmers cultivating myrtle, violet, rose and jasmine in the area of Grasse, a city located near Nice. The number of manufacturers exploded in the 19th century. Yet, in the nineteen sixties, European multinationals acquired many of them. Today, there are approximately seventy private businesses manufacturing flavours and fragrances, with a few of them established more than 50 years ago.

DOI: 10.4324/9780429281228-3

Among them, two have prospered and grown privately and independently. They respectively started their activity in 1850 and 1871, and in both firms the president is the fourth generation of owners running the business. With several thousand employees around the world and multiple subsidiaries, they have internationalized their activities, modernized their organization, and innovated. In the study, they appear with simple fictitious names: Essences and Aromas.

These family firms display strong values. They are proud of their savoir-faire, heritage, success, and communities. They are determined to preserve that heritage, to make it bear further fruit, and to transmit it to future generations. This paper proposes to examine how these values interact with their social responsibility and sustainability policies and practices.

It draws upon social identity theory and its role in the formation of values (Ashforth and Mael, 1989). Social identity theory has enabled researchers to better understand how individual identity and organizational identity intersect (Hatch and Schultz, 2002), a particularly relevant topic in this research given the significant influence that family members running their firms have on shaping organizational values (Astrachan, Klein, and Smyrnios, 2002). Then, the paper reviews the literature on values in CSR and more specifically how it is deployed in family businesses. The results characterize ethical values and behaviour in historic family firms, and the discussion looks at the way if affects sustainable behaviour.

Social Identity in Family Businesses

Social identity theory (SIT) speaks of 'family businesses' as socially hybrid organizations where the two distinct social categories of 'family' and 'business', may not respond to the same set of principles, values, and beliefs (Whetten, Foreman and Dyer, 2014). As organizations increasingly need to respond to a multitude of stakeholders, family businesses are more inclined to face both normative and utilitarian pressures. Some could argue that most organizations are hybrid, yet in family firms, hybridity lies at the purpose level, rather than at the managerial level of the firm. It signifies a greater salience of a dual perspective in family firms, where owners-managers have to consider societal and economic objectives in parallel and not independently. The reasons hold to certain characteristics of the two core identities, family, and business. When such characteristics are in conflict, they may seem 'incompatible', but research on family firms show that they remain 'indispensable' and 'inviolate' (Whetten, Foreman and Dyer, 2014, p. 486), as the expectations of stakeholders about those firms make it impossible for them to abandon some attributes to the benefit of others, a behaviour commonly found in public firms.

36 *Anne Barraquier*

It is therefore natural for family managers to protect and nurture the organization's identity. Albert and Whetten argued that an organization's identity is that which is central, enduring, and distinct. Identity becomes the reference set of values and beliefs in the face of conflictual decisions that managers must make about common business rationales and management principles (Shepherd and Haynie, 2009). In making such decisions, they sometimes play conflicting roles (family and manager) applying what appears to be conflicting rules. Identity connects the family and the organization. In a family business, the individual identity of founders irrigates the business organization, as the organization is an extension of them (Whetten, Foreman and Dyer, 2014). These two levels of analysis, individual and organizational, are therefore constantly interacting when examining issues of identity and promoted values (Hatch and Schultz, 2002).

In family businesses that persist for decades, if not centuries, the family managers inherit not just the business but also the knowledge of who is the 'family-organization' entity, what it represents in history, what it has endured and the fundamental attributes on which it has built its successes. They identify strongly with the organization that may bear their name and display a strong commitment to the preservation of the organization's identity. In historic firms, the enduring persistence of the organization signals the success of predecessors and enhances the obligation of success for the current manager. As a result, the owners of the next generation are brought up to consider the business organization as a second home, as a familiar extension of the family about which they have developed an emotional bond since childhood (Björnberg and Nicholson, 2012). This emotional relationship is built upon familiar people, locations, sites, products, and narratives that become constitutive of the identity of the future generation members. Such attributes of identity create a sense of purpose for the organization that goes beyond profit generation and economic interest at-large (Berrone et al., 2010). In family firms that involve several generations of owners, the family members, not restricted to the nuclear parent-child pattern, express a sense of belongingness to the same social group. The degree of cohesion and attachment between members of the group determines their identification with the social identity of the organization (Björnberg and Nicholson, 2012).

A Framework of Values in Business

CSR is defined as the ethical, social, and environmental policies that a business engages in beyond its legally required obligations (Griffin and Prakash, 2014). Previous research has shown that family-owned businesses do better than other firms on their social responsibility and environmental performance (Dyer and Whetten, 2006; Berrone et al., 2010). In their findings, researchers agree that the significance of the image and reputation of the firm for the owners leads them to engage in CSR, to commit to their stakeholders and to maintain high social and environmental standards. Besides, the emotional attachment of family owners to their firm reinforces their motivation to preserve the image of the firm, as it is an important part of their legacy. Conversely, publicly held corporations face institutional shareholders with no emotional ties, mostly seeking high returns (Berrone et al., 2010). In addition, research has shown that the ethical commitment of the top management implies a better integration of CSR policies in the firm, whereas CSR introduced by formal programs tends to be decoupled from real practices (Weaver, Trevino and Cochran, 1999). Such commitment is an attribute more frequent in family firms, where ethical values are constitutive of the firm's identity. This assumption has driven scholars to explore values in family businesses, and to understand how values connect to CSR.

William Frederick has provided one of the most appealing approaches to the concept of 'values' in business ethics. In his book, *"Values, Nature and Culture in the American Corporation"* (1995), he argues that three sets of values, or "value clusters", are competing within firms, an incompatibility that is the source of the tension between business and society (Frederick, 1995). For Frederick (1995) a value can be defined as a belief, a relationship, a judgment and an experience. He draws from Rokeach's seminal definition to define a value as "an enduring belief that a specific mode of conduct or end-state of existence is personally or socially preferable to an opposite or converse mode of conduct" (Rokeach, 1973, cited by Frederick, 1995, p. 16). A value is therefore cognitive. It also has an affective dimension. A value can be seen in relationships among individuals. Indeed, values have a meaning when they are shared and observed by others (Frederick, 1995). 'Value' also refers to judgment since it involves an evaluation to determine whether something is valuable. Finally, and importantly, values come from a variety of experiences made by human beings. Experiences shape values. Therefore, values are the outcome of experience and in that sense, they become important components of our identities.

Frederick (1995) provides a framework based on three value clusters present in business organizations. 'Economizing values' promote economic efficiency, 'ecologizing values' seek social and ecological welfare, and 'power aggrandizement values' drive top management to accumulate and retain coercive power. This framework is relevant to discuss CSR engagement in different contexts. It conceptualizes the interaction of the three 'value clusters'. Public or private governance, family or non-family ownership can create heterogeneity in organizational behaviour. In such different shareholding contexts, patterns of interaction between the different value sets may differ. For instance, agency theory has shown that in public companies, 'economizing values', favourable to shareholders, compete with 'power aggrandizement' values of management executives.

38   *Anne Barraquier*

Thus, firms' engagement in social responsibility can be predicated upon specific patterns of tension between the different value sets and promoted by the salience of one value set over the others.

Frederick (1995) argues that 'economizing values' are compatible with 'ecologizing values', because economizing processes seek the optimal and most efficient use of resources, an objective consistent with ecological welfare. Conversely, the quest to aggrandize their power leads executives to misuse economic resources and hamper ecologising processes. Power-focused values diverge from economic and ecological values in several ways. They create social barriers between the power holders and the rest of the communities internal and external to the organization. They drive managers to make decisions favourable to the enlargement of their power to the detriment of the rational needs of the organization. For instance, power-seeking executives (or board members) tend to adopt acquisition policies rather than organic growth policies, because acquisitions rapidly increase their power sphere while organic growth gradually delivers benefits. They also use the quest of economizing values towards shareholders to justify their power increase strategies. In addition, those seeking power highly value status rank, which appears in different symbolic artefacts such as, "clothing, manner of address, precedence in speaking during meetings, seating order, location and size of office, quality of office furnishings, pay and diverse perquisites, and other such features of the workplace" (Frederick, 1995, p. 61).

Family members running their firms exert a significant influence on shaping organizational values (Astrachan, Klein, and Smyrnios, 2002). Since all family firms, as hybrid organizations, need to reconcile the capacities of the organization to be efficient in using resources ('economizing') and to remain morally virtuous ('ecologizing'), the role of the values promoted by the family as a business, strongly affects stakeholder behaviour. Employees need to adopt these values in the conduct of their mission to keep their position in the organization, suppliers must comply with those values to continue their business with the organization, and customers 'buy' the values together with the products and services delivered by the organization.

In most non-family business organizations, the efficiency rationale and the economization of resources to increase profit remain the core mission of the business. The relationship with and impact on society are conveyed through the business processes, not the mission or purpose. The extent to which they become included in the process should not alter the process efficiency in its quest to fulfil its essential mission, which is to maximise profits for shareholders. In fact, the original values of business drive it to economize resources, grow the business and respect the integrity of the business system. As we have seen, these values are in reality compatible with social, societal and ecological values (Frederick, 1995), but power aggrandizement prevents that cohesion.

Conversely, in long-lasting family-owned businesses, studies show that the cohesion of social and economic values seems less problematic (Dyer and Whetten, 2006) than in other firms. In non-family firms, this difficulty may be related to the enduring belief that the "only social responsibility of the firm is to make profit". This paradigm has prevailed so far in management studies, to the point where the maximisation of shareholder value. Conversely, family businesses make constant efforts to conciliate social and economic objectives. As old family firms' owners greatly care about their family firm social identity, their concern about the preservation of their name does not allow them to neglect social and ecological issues. Even if publicly traded, they continue to take into account the communities among which they have been long established, and to preserve their employees, long-time suppliers and other partners. That said, social science research has discovered very little about the behavioural processes that could be at play, the social dynamics that could explain how and in what ways family businesses enact the conciliation of economic and ecological objectives.

To follow Frederick's steps, the paper proposes to look at the way individuals experience ethical values and enact ethical behaviour in their organization. It explores, through a qualitative study, the way organization members conceive and experience ethical behaviour in their activities. There are two related research questions:

- how do presidents (owners) of a historic family firm conceive ethical behaviour and underpinning values?
- How do managers in a historic family firm experience ethical behaviour and ethical values?

Methods

This study is part of a larger qualitative research project which examined how social responsibility was shared among members of the organization. Although the interview protocol included some questions about corporate values, many informants spontaneously discussed them in relation to the family ownership. Therefore, the questions did not much refer to 'values' explicitly, which enabled the researcher to capture unbiased accounts about how values are reflected in CSR. These accounts produced data on the perception of the family values in the two firms and revealed new insights about the interaction of different sets of values, and about the importance of ethics and responsibility within promoted values. Before presenting the details of the qualitative study, I briefly introduce both family businesses.

ESSENCES is a publicly-traded corporation, where the family members still hold a majority stake. They seem to be eager to keep it this way. A recent press interview with the president (I call him Bob in this paper)

40   *Anne Barraquier*

reported that his grandfather had sold so many shares to external partners that his father devoted his entire life to regain the majority and restore his family legacy. When Bob inherited the responsibility to run the business, he put a strong emphasis on the long-term preservation of Essences, and he is now involved in preparing the next generation in learning the technique of the business as much as the commercial part. Essences annual sales are around six hundred million dollars and has more than two thousand employees in the world. Bob is the fourth generation of owners.

AROMAS is private and has never been publicly traded. The current president, Max, is also representing the fifth generation, and just like Bob in Essences, he is working with the new generation to let them take over in a few years. In all press interviews, Max insists on the importance of preserving the private governance of the firm. Annual sales at Aromas reach approximately 1.3 billion dollars, with six thousand employees worldwide. Both companies have historic headquarters in the southeast of France, with multiple subsidiaries at the international level. They both specialize in natural flavours and fragrances and less in synthetic and artificial compounds.

The paper presents the analysis of twenty-one interviews conducted in ESSENCES and AROMAS. I interviewed the two presidents first. At the end of the interview, I collected names of managers likely to respond to questions about social responsibility in the organization. After I met each of them, they provided me with other relevant contacts, and so on. During my presence in the organization, the managers I interviewed provided me with numerous documents such as internal memos, copies of emails, product-related documentation, prints of computer screens, internal policies documents, etc. I also searched the internet to find interviews of the two presidents. In the press, family firms tend to emphasize values and identity issues as a way to enhance the reputation of their firm, but also to capture the attention of journalists. In qualitative studies, it is important to collect data from written text sources to strengthen the validity of interview data (Yin, 2003).

Interviewing the president first allowed me to capture his vision of social responsibility, of what it meant for him. In both firms, the presidents expressed a very personal, critical, and unconventional vision of CSR. In these circumstances, the interpretation and appropriation of that vision by managers becomes particularly interesting. Thus, the unit of analysis is dual, with the president owners as those who disseminate and the managers who are recipients. We thought the dual unit was crucial, as family firms do not dissociate ownership and management.

To analyse the data, I used the Nvivo qualitative analysis software. Nvivo enables researchers to code very close to the text, to identify emerging themes. These first-order codes (Gioia, Schultz and Corley, 2000; Gioia, Corley and Hamilton, 2013) produce a detailed analysis of the data.

Then, researchers analyse, organize, and categorize the first-order codes into a second-level categorization of second-order themes. This second level helps the researcher to conceptualize theoretical insights and build theory.

Findings

Findings are summarized in Table 2.1. The summary presents the analysis of the coded interviews and press releases. It reflects the categorization of the data analysis done according to the Gioia methodology for inductive research, with first-order themes, second-order themes, and

Table 2.1 Data Structure

First Order Themes	*Second-Order Themes*	*Aggregate Dimensions*
• Acting not talking • Implicit organizing • Implicit and not measurable values • Informal CSR	Contesting explicit rules Ethical values are experienced	Embedded Ethics
• Lack of communication • Strategy is not easily perceived • Difficult for newcomers to fit in • Soft hierarchy boundaries	Opacity Complex organisation	Learning by doing
• Success rests on individual initiative • Individuals should act for the company • People before organisation • Long term interest of the employees	Employees contribute Organisation cares	Implicit mutual interest
• The President is involved in work meetings • The President works hard • The President is physically present • The President is accessible to all	Working 'among' not 'above Personal relation is possible	Anchored power
• Family invests locally • The local roots of the family is promoted • Families of employees are employed through generations • The firm is involved with local communities	Local attachment Local involvement	Grounded stewardship
• Corporate citizenship as identity • Relations founded on respect • The company has a soul • Ethics is about going further	Social engagement is natural Company as a moral person	Natural moral sense
• Family ownership ensures continuity • Family/public long term perspective • Family ownership long term relations • Continuity is a value	Family is a guardian Sustainability is systemic	Guardians of sustainability

42 *Anne Barraquier*

aggregate dimensions. To enable a better understanding of the first-order themes that emerged from coding the data very closely, the paper includes a second table (Table 2.2) in the appendix section, containing one or two exemplary quotes for each theme.

Seven aggregate dimensions have emerged: embedded ethics, learning by doing, implicit mutual interest, anchored power, grounded stewardship, natural moral sense, and guardians of sustainability. All dimensions reflect a preference for a mode of action which follows tacit rules rather than explicit conventions and articulated communication. 'Embedded ethics' describes the consistency between the way these family businesses implicitly organize activity processes and convey moral conduct and values. 'Learning by doing' shows the implications of such tacitness on communication and behaviour, and the necessity for individuals to experience the corporate culture to understand it and fit it. As a result, people manage to produce benefits for the organization, and the company makes sure it acts for their interest in the long term, producing a virtuous effect of 'implicit mutual interest'. In that context, employees consider the family owners to represent 'an anchored power' that has a reassuring and stabilizing effect on their work. They are prompt to praise the engagement of the firm locally ('grounded stewardship') and its attachment to the land and the communities living there. When asked to think about the ethics of the company, employees report a normal way to do things, with respect, as if the company had a 'natural moral sense' that needed to be applied as much and as far as possible. Finally, the vision for the future that owners share makes them appear as guardians with a duty to protect what has been built before them and to make it prosper for them and the communities.

Embedded Ethics

In both firms, family owners describe the CSR policies in public firms (with dissociated ownership and management unlike Essences where the family has a majority stake) as "a reference system which after all, is just about indicators" (top manager, Essences). They mock CSR standards, which according to them only formalize a conduct that their firms have always maintained and that large public corporations just pay lip service to. They oppose the standardization of CSR as well as the discourse to promote CSR, insisting that ethical conduct should be quietly promoted through action and not through talk.

For the family owners, ethical conduct, whether it concerns the relations with stakeholders, work relations or environmental issues, is part of a more systemic approach to firm activities organizing. They handle ethical conduct in the business similarly to other types of activity processes such as management and strategy processes. Organizational charts and strategic plans are not systematically made explicit. When they exist,

Sustainability in Historic Family Firms   43

they are not a very important reference document. What matters is the way things have always been done: with honesty and respect.

For the two presidents interviewed as well as their top managers, the values are there, deeply rooted in the history and the culture of the organization. That culture has emerged from a peasant ancestry, great-grandfathers who cultivated flowers to produce essential oils. As one HR manager with a long history with Aromas said, "when a farmer has to go working in the fields, he doesn't say 'I'm going to work in the fields', he just goes to work in the fields". The metaphor was used to illustrate the registration of the company to the Global Compact U.N principles in 2005. The president of Aromas didn't want to mention it on the company's brochures or newsletter, as a marketing device. This type of reluctance could be found in a number of other situations.

Tacit values are anchored, customary and difficult to express. They appear in various, sometimes unexpected circumstances, which makes it difficult to integrate them into formal CSR policies, and to fit a conventional CSR agenda. This may be difficult to understand by some managers because they tend to dissociate the social, ethical and environmental concerns from the economic purpose of the organization, whereas the president sees it as a whole. A business unit manager, who had been a top executive at one of the public competitors, was bewildered to see that the company hired disabled workers despite their lower productivity while many businesses preferred to pay the 'disability tax'.

Learning by Doing

People working and representing the firm should understand how to act without having to be taught. Rather, they are encouraged to experience the culture. In the same way, they should perform their tasks in a loose structure and hierarchy. The two firms are proud to explain that processes are quite efficient and responsive, conversely to larger, publicly held corporations where a rigid hierarchy is dehumanizing and inefficient.

Admirable, but also problematic. Tacit values are more difficult to share and disseminate than explicit values. As a result, managers often complain about the lack of communication, or the absence of a clear strategy. They never blame the boss but blame the top managers. They excuse their president because he cannot be ubiquitous but comment on top managers who do not communicate enough. Indeed, the human resources manager at Aromas, glorifies the peasant family who is not contaminated by the "verbal diarrhoea" of public companies' CEOs. In both companies, the absence of communication is voluntary. One subscribed to the U.N Global Compact principles but refused to commodify this type of engagement in its marketing policies. They buy organic raw materials to manufacture their products but do not use them as a commercial argument. Salespeople

44 *Anne Barraquier*

become frustrated because they see social engagement as proper marketing tools, but their president says "this is marketing for idiots" (Table 2.2). For individuals, the organization can be a complex web of relations. The absence of explicit processes, charts, codes of conduct compels newcomers to adopt the culture quickly to navigate comfortably and some fail. As an H.R manager admitted, "we prefer to discourage them to see how far they are ready to go to adopt our culture". That culture implies that organization members accept rules and values to become part of the group.

Implicit Mutual Interest

Informants discuss mutual interest as a reciprocal contract between the employees who must contribute, and the organization that should take care of them. One could argue that this sounds like a common engagement in any type of organization. However, in these firms, it has a strong affective and emotional dimension. In short, the organization expects employees to be representatives of the company and to act for the company as if it was theirs. One of the two presidents expressed nostalgia about the time of his father, when the employees used to feel part of a big family and take part in celebrations organized by the company. He said that he enjoyed travelling to Asia or South America because there, people were "eager to know what they can do for the company" (Table 2.2). An extreme example is one comment of a general manager who complained about the regulatory affairs manager to often take side with the regulator and not acting in the interest of the company and adding that they were proud to have succeeded in hiring him from a competitor, because he was very competent!

In both businesses, managers insist on the importance of business performance, sales, and profitability. However, Essences emphasizes profitability differently than Aromas does. Being publicly traded, they insist that even though the firm is family-owned, the financial markets help keeping an eye on profitability. In a way, they justify being publicly traded, as if they were scared to be blamed for going public as a family company. Conversely, in Aromas, profitability is important, but when people mention it, they insist that profitability is about investment and also, that the company does not make hasty decisions.

In both firms, managers value the stability that they enjoy in the company where stock market fluctuations may affect the activity but do not have immediate impacts. In almost two hundred years, neither of the two firms had a collective redundancy or layoff plan motivated by economic reasons. One business unit director, who had worked for a publicly listed competitor, was amazed at the unawareness of employees concerning the hard reality of competitive employment in public multinationals and concluded, "they just don't know anything about that". Working conditions are good, people matter. Whether the informants were in the top management or plain executives, they reported equally that they were being taken care of. One top manager argued that the absence of an organizational chart was since "people come before the organization". The family owners are eager to keep relations simple and want people to be able to contact anybody they want in the organization, without a strict hierarchy keeping individuals in silos. Interestingly, when questions focused on CSR, the fair treatment of employees was often the first issue that came to the mind of the informants. Respect was recurrently mentioned in the interviews. It concerned the respect the family has for the employees but also the respect as a value that the family requests from the employees to the stakeholders.

Anchored Power

Managers described the behaviour of the president (owner-manager) in different ways. He is hard-working, responsive, dedicated, and accessible. He is admired for this commitment to the company even though it might seem natural, if he is a major shareholder. Managers nevertheless recognize his devotion, wondering sometimes how he can do so much in one day. They also value his presence in meetings where they can call upon his expertise, and his engagement in action when tough issues arise. They see him as someone working among them, not apart from them, and not above the organization.

The president is seldom criticized, conversely to his top management. Yet, one area of critique is unambiguously the lack of communication described in a previous section. Both presidents are viewed as responsible for the absence of exchange and explanations inside the organization. Informants connect that fault to the identity of the business – and therefore, the family – imbued with discretion and humility in discourse. But in parallel, they praise his physical presence that can occur anywhere on the manufacturing site. They interpret the strong messages of that 'bodily' presence. For instance, one manager is ecstatic about how his president knows the plant in every nook and cranny. Several insist that they are lucky not to have a multitude of anonymous shareholders making decisions for the company and a CEO distributing dividends. They feel reassured that the president and his family members are real, physical people that they all personally know, that they can talk to solve problems and invest in the company. Employees know who makes decisions, power is incarnated, as everyone talks to the boss once in a while. Recurrent testimonies converged to say that anyone could go to the president's office and bypass their management. One top manager even said that when this happened, he had to go to the bypassed manager to repair it. The personal relation with and the presence of the president characterize this context as "anchored power". Deep roots that the

46 *Anne Barraquier*

family has developed in the land of origin nurtures power anchoring, driving it to display a 'grounded stewardship'.

Grounded Stewardship

The two studied firms provide recurrent examples of the significance of investments made locally to grow the local activity, extend facilities, and develop R&D to anchor innovation locally. This dimension is not only "promoted" by the presidents, but it also literally emerges in the interviews of managers (the interview protocol did not have questions about this issue). They are proud to share that information with outsiders. One environmental affairs manager expressed real joy at the perspective of very expensive equipment that the company had just decided to invest in, an investment which was crucial to drastically increase the environmental performance of the firm. The owners justify the investment by their attachment to the place where the company was founded. It is the place where they were born and grew up. The place makes it possible for them to connect the successful past to the future of the company. The temporal continuity exists because it is strongly related to an identified place which guarantees the attributes of the organizational identity.

The family also get locally involved. First, it seeks to demonstrate its attachment to the families of the employees, who for some of them, have work there from generation to generation. Informants report about the importance for the company to keep up with the tradition of hiring the children of employees. In both firms, this is a common pattern. A manager, having joined the firm at a late stage of his career, confessed that he first found it upsetting (maybe other people would be more competent), but gradually came to consider that it was positive because it reflected strong values. In press interviews, both presidents argued that they strived to keep the family business going because the firm was an important employer in the local community.

Second, for the family, the local communities go beyond the employed families. Both firms are important actors of local life and contribute to tax, employment, and activity. Therefore, they care to respond to the claims of local stakeholders, such as the neighbouring communities, the authorities of towns and villages around them, associations, and NGOs. They actively participate in economic activity, helping and financing trade associations and training institutes. Finally, they get involved in charitable activities, and contribute to solving social issues that emerge in their local environment.

Natural Moral Sense

The results showed striking convergence of managers who described the extent to which ethics was the right way to do things and to act towards stakeholders. It was amusing to see that each company had a word for it. Aroma's managers resorted easily to "ethics" as "the way we do things", and the words "ethics" and "ethical" were frequent in their discourse. A chemist told a story about an "ethical molecule", saying that he was first puzzled and had to ask Max what he meant by that, until he could translate it into more technical terms. Sometimes managers complained about what they viewed as a quite radical perspective from their president. A sales manager in charge of the European clients' accounts explained that he found himself in situations where he felt he had to be the "white knight" when the outside world was unethical.

At Essences, several people mentioned "respect" as a natural behaviour that everyone agreed upon and observed. People mentioned "respect" as a value or as a behaviour. A respectful behaviour was for them what characterized the guiding principles they followed when dealing with suppliers, customers, local stakeholders.

Both companies portrayed ethics and respect as something that personified the company. A number of quotations about ethical behaviour started with "us". These statements differed from those where managers spoke of situations they confronted as an individual manager. They clearly expressed a sense of common good, of belongingness to the larger group, to the organization. The organization seemed to be a moral person; an entity triggered by one motto. Ethical behaviour is a collective engagement shared by all, and it is a duty to go beyond the regulative compliance, because the "company has a soul". Managers and presidents do not, in the interviews, connect the idea of being good to the ideas of competitiveness, reputation or legitimacy. The presidents and family members certainly know about the possible advantage of good behaviour, but the data collected clearly shows that they want to disconnect ethical behaviour from any kind of gain. Ethical (respectful) behaviour should reflect the identity of the firm.

Guardians of Sustainability

In these two historic family firms, owners display a sense of responsibility for the perpetuation of the firm and of its activities. As their company has proven successful across generations, they perceive their own role not just as the new generation entrepreneurs but as heirs of a precious legacy that should be preserved. In a sense, current owners have not only inherited a business, but they have also inherited the history, the values, the business principles, partnerships, and relations. Their responsibility is not just social and economic, but also cultural, experiential, and relational. Although it is well accepted that each new generation imprints its own way, it does not stray from the cultural roadmap established by previous generations and is reflected in the corporate identity. Value sets and cultural norms are part of the legacy.

48 *Anne Barraquier*

They can be expressed differently, but they sustain. This is why, in the study, the two current presidents express a profound attachment to the history of their firms and easily refer to their future. For instance, Bob, the president of Essences hopes that "the company is still here in three centuries, in its historical site" and that his "family still runs it". In a press interview, Max, Aromas's president, explains the significance of the integration of the new generation members in the company to ensure the positive continuity of the business.

In addition, the firm insists on the importance to maintain and nurture long-term trusting relations with stakeholders. Both firms have for instance developed strong partnerships with suppliers of raw materials all over the world. Of course, as both firms specialize in the manufacturing of natural products, it is important for them to secure quality sourcing. Nevertheless, when questioned about the firm's relationship with suppliers, some managers nodded and said, "we are nice clients. We really are the nice guys". Others expressed deep respect towards clients, and ethical behaviour widely shared at Essences (see "natural moral sense" section) within all departments and services of the organization. Some partnerships date back several decades and were signed by the previous generation of owners. All in all, the value of continuity is part of the moral behaviour of the firm. Through the preservation of the business relations, the identity of the family business reaches out to other groups. Continuity of the business does not just apply to the organization itself but also to the socio-economic system it belongs to.

Discussion and Conclusion

Previous literature has identified the superior sustainability performance of family firms over publicly traded firms, as well as the significance of values as a determinant of firm longevity. It has also been interested to identify the values at play, to rank and measure values, and to assess the importance of ethics and social responsibility among values (Tàpies and Fernández Moya, 2012) while other studies have looked at the role of values in CSR engagement (Marques, Presas and Simon, 2014). To our knowledge, there is no prior research, on how owners and organization members conceive, perceive and experience ethical values. Previous studies have not focused on these perceptions and experiences.

The discussion section aims at defining our contribution to theory. It unfolds in two parts. First, it looks at the tacit nature of ethical behaviour in historic family firms in its various dimensions, and it examines the temporal, spatial and systemic continuity. Second, these grounded social dynamics are discussed as explanatory of social and ecological sustainability through the lens of Frederick's framework of values. It suggests that the data implies a reduced 'power aggrandizement' value

Sustainability in Historic Family Firms   49

cluster in family firms, which could explain that economic and ecological values are more likely to coexist.

Tacitness and Grounded, Systemic Continuity

In numerous studies on CSR, researchers look at brochures, websites, and other codified information to understand the involvement of organizations in CSR and sustainability activities. In contrast, our study unveils a more tacit practice of ethics. Indeed, the analysis of the findings reveals the experiential and naturalistic nature of ethical values and behaviour. It sheds light on the tacit nature of ethical values and sustainable practices rather than examining their implicit expression. Our findings connect with former studies which depicted values of modesty, sobriety, and humility (Tàpies and Fernández Moya, 2012) as foundational in family firms, which contrasts with the discourse-based behaviour of publicly listed firms claiming CSR policies, a strategy viewed as manipulative and as a quest for legitimacy (Scherer, Palazzo and Seidl, 2013).

In this paper, we found in the verbatim of the two owners and their managers that the testimonies reflected values commonly found in old family firms. Among those values, honesty, sobriety and humility are among the most highly ranked (Tàpies and Fernández Moya, 2012). The results show that the reluctance to ostentation (Table 2.2, in "acting not talking"), a form of sobriety, justifies the contest of any attempt to use ethical behaviour as a utility. Thus, these underlying values capture – in the truest sense of the word – ethical behaviour. They won't let it become an abstract and discursive device serving communication and marketing but rather, these underpinning values embed ethics in deeds. As shown in the categorization of the results, ethics are tacitly experienced in various ways. The organization engages in CSR activity but does not discuss it. Employees learn ethical ways "by doing", and not by a code of conduct. The owners display a physical connection to their facilities, activities and employees. The moral sense of the organization is natural and not codified. The family members act for their communities through the quiet relationship to their common land and common history. The relationship of the family to ethical behaviour is tacit, grounded and in a way, naturalistic.

To defend their naturalistic perspective, Lincoln and Guba (1985, page 195) explain that, "it is not possible to describe or explain everything that one 'knows' in language form; some things must be experienced to be understood". Some would argue that the firm does not capitalize on responsible behaviour for its reputation and image (as shown in the results, this lack of communication vexes employees). Others would also say that the firm's most salient stakeholders do not have a clear perception of the firm's actions and policies. Such implications may be true. However, this naturalistic approach to ethics may also

50 Anne Barraquier

be explanatory of the better sustainability performance of these businesses. After all, sustainability audits examine facts, not discourses.

The second aspect of the tacit nature of ethics in historic family firms is their grounded character which comes from their local anchorage, their ancient origin and their holistic perception of ethical duties. Of course, the territorial belongingness may occasionally serve as a promoting tool for the firm, to recruit or to legitimize the firm's activities towards local communities and other stakeholders. The ancient roots of the firm are mentioned in various presentations of the firm. Finally, the systemic perspective appears in websites and other communication and reporting devices. Roots, history and ecosystems are present in most firms' narratives because they represent fundamental knowledge that the modern world of consumption demands from commercial businesses.

Yet, individuals in organizations rarely discuss the intrinsic ethical character of spatial, temporal and systemic dimensions because they perceive these dimensions as organizational structures and symbolic institutions that contain a concrete form of knowledge. Social identity literature explains that succeeding generations of owners in family businesses display an emotional attachment to their business firm, a sense of ownership that is "a matter of sentiment, associated with belongingness and attachment beyond the monetary significance of the ownership bond, in which the family had a central role" (Björnberg and Nicholson, 2012). Such attachment translates into an imperative of ethical behaviour conveyed by owners, experienced by organization members, and perceived by other stakeholders. Historical roots and local anchoring of these firms are symbolic institutions, and as such, they have the power to structure behaviour and social dynamics in an organization.

Barriers to Power Aggrandizement

Frederick (1995) indicated in his value-clusters framework that economizing values could be compatible with ecologising values. In short, in economizing resources to generate profit, firms also economize sustainability factors such as energy and raw materials. In addition, the capacity provided to employees to be happy at work has positive impacts and generate returns. Frederick (1995) specified, however, that the third cluster played a negative role in this compatibility. The quest for power aggrandizement "leads executives to misuse economic resources and hamper ecologizing processes". Frederick saw four different power aggrandizement values: hierarchical organization, managerial decision making, power-system equilibrium and power aggrandizement.

The organization of the firm as a hierarchy generates power tensions and struggles, where managers tend to spend their resources and energy in the preservation of their prerogatives and not to the service of the organization and with authority towards others. Frederick specifies that this form of authority arises in the absence of the natural ownership authority. As a result, managers tend to make decisions (i.e acquisitions, strategic priorities, dismissals...) which are in favour of their managerial needs. This generates a distance, and social barriers between them and their employees as well as other stakeholders. Yet, they need to preserve an equilibrium as too much-concentrated power could become illegitimate, creating a rupture that can threaten the whole system of power they are in. Preserving the system is important to safeguard oneself in the system, and most of all to keep one's social status and prestige which appears through a variety of material symbols, such as status, material display of wealth, luxurious office, high position in different business circumstances. Finally, the expansion of the business favours the expansion of power and status of managers.

In family businesses, the tacitness of ethical engagement may be a barrier to power aggrandizement. When modesty and humility are values applied by the family owners, it becomes more difficult to brag about one's success or hegemony. Every manager knows where the real power is, and the representation of power is anchored and physical. The reluctance to the ostentation of family members is not compatible with the need of the status of power-seeking managers. Economizing resources is an imperative in historic family firms, who will not permit lavish behaviour. In historic firms, the strong control on how things are done in the business limits self-oriented managerial behaviour. It examines closely at the highest level (family owners) acquisition and other growth projects. Unlike what happens in publicly traded firms, the managers cannot align their interest in this regard with the CEO's, in the back of shareholders. To conclude, in historic family firms, the significance of power aggrandizement values traditionally present in public firms are considerably diminished where the tacit nature of ethics impede the development of this managerial behaviour.

Limits and Conclusion

Our paper seeks to contribute to a better understanding of the superior sustainability performance of family firms. It introduces the idea that power aggrandizement can be a source of irresponsibility in non-family firms because ethics is disseminated in a more explicit and abstract manner. The naturalistic approach of old family firms to ethics enables them to defuse the attempts of managers to seek more power and thereby creates a more favourable environment for the coexistence of profit and ethics.

Our study is nonetheless limited by the exploratory character of the investigation which does not allow the generalization of results. It creates, however, opportunities for further empirical studies to test our results, and opens avenues of research on the forms that tacit ethics can take in organizations.

References

Anderson, R.C. and Reeb, D.M. (2003) 'Founding-family ownership and firm performance: evidence from the S&P 500', *The Journal of Finance*, 58(3), pp. 1301–1328.

Ashforth, B. and Mael, F. (1989) 'Social identity theory and the organization', *Academy of Management Review*, 14, pp. 20–39.

Astrachan, J.H., Klein, S.B. and Smyrnios, K.X. (2002) 'The F-PEC scale of family influence: A proposal for solving the family business definition problem', *Family Business Review*, 15(1), pp. 45–58.

Berrone, P. *et al.* (2010) 'Socioemotional wealth and corporate responses to institutional pressures: Do family-controlled firms pollute less?' *Administrative Science Quarterly*, 55(1), pp. 82–113.

Björnberg, Å. and Nicholson, N. (2012) 'Emotional ownership: The next generation's relationship with the family firm', *Family Business Review*, 25(4), pp. 374–390.

Dyer, Jr W.G. and Whetten, D.A. (2006) 'Family firms and social responsibility: Preliminary evidence from the S&P 500', *Entrepreneurship Theory and Practice*, 30(6), pp. 785–802.

Frederick, W. (1995) *Values, nature and culture in the American Corporation*. New York: Oxford University Press.

Gioia, D.A., Schultz, M. and Corley, K. (2000) 'Organizational identity, image, and adaptive instability', *Academy of Management Review*, 25(1), pp. 63–81.

Gioia, D.A., Corley, K.G. and Hamilton, A.L. (2013) ' Seeking qualitative rigor in inductive research: Notes on the Gioia methodology'. *Organizational Research Methods*, 16(1), pp. 15–31.

Griffin, J.J. and Prakash, A. (2014) 'Corporate responsibility: Initiatives and mechanisms', *Business & Society*, 53(4), pp. 465–482.

Hatch, M.J. and Schultz, M. (2002) 'The dynamics of organizational identity', *Human Relations*, 55, pp. 989–1018.

Korainen, M., (2002) 'Over 100 years of age but still entrepreneurially active in business: Exploring the values and family characteristics of old Finnish family firms', *Family Business Review*, 15(3), pp. 175–187.

Lincoln, Y.S. and Guba, E.G. (1985) *Naturalistic inquiry*. SAGE.

Scherer, A.G., Palazzo, G. and Seidl, D. (2013) 'Managing legitimacy in complex and heterogeneous environments: Sustainable development in a globalized world', *Journal of Management Studies*, 50(2), pp. 259–284.

Shepherd, D. and Haynie, J.M. (2009) 'Family business, identity conflict, and an expedited entrepreneurial process: A process of resolving identity conflict', *Entrepreneurship Theory & Practice*, 33(6), pp. 1245–1264.

Tàpies, J. and Fernández Moya, M. (2012) 'Values and longevity in family business: Evidence from a cross-cultural analysis', *Journal of Family Business Management*, 2(2), pp. 130–146.

Weaver, G.R., Trevino, L.K. and Cochran, P.L. (1999) 'Integrated and decoupled corporate social performance: Management commitments, external pressures, and corporate ethics practices', *Academy of Management Journal*, 42(5), pp. 539–552.

Whetten, D., Foreman, P. and Dyer, W.G. (2014) Organizational identity and family business. *The SAGE handbook of family business*, pp. 480–497.

Yin, R.K. (2003) 'Case study research design and methods third edition', *Applied Social Research Methods Series*, 5, pp. 228–231.

Appendix

Table 2.2 Exemplary Quotes

Exemplary quotes	Themes
EMBEDDED ETHICS	
"I want prayer rooms in our facilities in Indonesia, but not to be ostentatious. I don't want ostentation" (CEO)"we want to be acting good, not to be looking good" (HR manager)	Acting not talking
" we don't have organization charts" (general manager)"Here we are in a very flexible and responsive system, where you can ask anything to anyone in the company and it's very efficient" (Business unit manager)	Implicit organizing
"Getting rid of 15 or 20 people because of lower profits doesn't exist here. Employees don't know, they don't even have a clue about such things… and curiously the company doesn't capitalize on this" (Business Unit manager)	Implicit and not measurable values
"I don't want sales people to take advantage of the fact that we buy organic vanilla. This is marketing for idiots. Let's go back to common sense". (CEO)"We have two girls with a disability who fold the sniff stickers, you know, for perfume. Well, it's not efficient but it's a moral responsibility. Other companies prefer to pay a fine [instead of hiring disabled workers]. (Business unit manager)	Informal CSR
LEARNING BY DOING	
"It's obvious, there is a communication deficit (…) between Max and the rest of the organization" (Reg.affairs manager)"Paradoxically there is still an oral tradition in this company but as we grow it becomes difficult" (Quality manager)	Lack of communication
"we do a lot of good things but we don't communicate about the good things that we do" (Quality manager)	Strategy is not easily perceived
"Because of its long history, Aromas has a very strong culture. Newcomers either take it or leave it"	Difficulty of newcomers to fit in
You may have noticed but hierarchy is a very blurred and soft concept here at Essences (Business unit manager)	Soft hierarchy boundaries
IMPLICIT MUTUAL INTEREST	
"I love going to our subsidiaries in China or India, people there are grateful and eager to	Success rests on individual intiative

(Continued)

54 Anne Barraquier

Table 2.2 (Continued)

Exemplary quotes	Themes
know what they can do for the company" (President)	
"On environmental issues there is Mr X, he's a real messiah, he preaches the good word and would come in hell with me" (President)	Employees should act for the company
"Hierarchy does not matter much. Here people come before the organization" (general manager)	People before the organization
"Bob says 'I make decisions favorable to employees on the long term', but this is not necessarily well understood"	Long term interest of the employees
ANCHORED POWER	
"We have a meeting and we discuss that we could do like this for instance, and Max will be here too and we're all together" (Quality manager)	The president is involved in work meetings
"I'm lucky that my boss is very present, I don't know when he sleeps, he has a phenomenal work capacity" (Reg. affairs manager)	The president works hard
"He can take you anywhere in the plant facilities, can show you a pipe, tell you why it's there and where it goes" (Environmental affairs manager)	The president is physically present
If someone, an order picker wants an appointment with Bob (president), he gets it. That's how we manage things.	The president is accessible to all
GROUNDED SENSE OF STEWARDSHIP	
"The family members, their name is the name of the company. They invest and they get involved" (Quality manager)	Family invests locally
"Our local roots are old and deep. My grandfather was picking flowers here, he built the company in this village where our headquarters still are" (president)	Local roots of the family is promoted
"He's the son of the former production manager. Here at Aromas, families are many!" (Quality manager)	Families of employees are employed through generations
"the family lives here in the city, they know the children and the grandchildren of the families. They feel responsible for these people who were hired because they fit with the corporate culture" (General manager)	The firm is involved with local communities
NATURAL MORAL SENSE	
"We are a citizen. We do a lot" (Quality manager) "For us ethics is the normal way to do things" (President)	Corporate citizenship as identity

(Continued)

Sustainability in Historic Family Firms 55

Table 2.2 (Continued)

Exemplary quotes	Themes
"Ethics here is about respect. Respect of the customer, of external stakeholders, of the different cultural contexts we work in" (general manager)"We are not very good at communicating within the company, but respect is important here. It's part of us." (Quality manager)	Relations grounded on respect
"Responsibility must be held. We are lucky to have a soul. Aromas has a soul because it has roots and a strong culture" (HR manager)	The company has a soul
"I consider that when we have freedom of choice, we must go beyond standards for the natural environment" (president)	Ethics is about going further
GUARDIANS OF SUSTAINABILIY	
"I would be happy to know that the company is still here in three centuries, in its historical site and that my family still runs it" (president)"Max doesn't have a short term vision. He cares about profitability of course, but what he wants is to make his plant sustainable" (Reg.affairs manager)	Family ownership ensures continuity
"In terms of performance over the long term, the majority stake of the family provides the means and ensures stability" (general manager)	Public&family owned: long term perspective
"the family dimension allows stability, and therefore long term relations with our partners" (general manager)	Family ownership long term relations
"The company belongs to the family and that's a strength. It enables us to have a long term strategy and guarantee the stability" (president's son)"As the company is not publicly traded, my policy has been to distribute almost no dividend and to massively invest, to increase R&D spending and to hire people" (president).	Continuity is a value

3 Employees Returns on "Ramadan Packages" as a Corporate Social Responsibility Practice: Moderating Role of Perceived Corporate Sincerity

Erhan Boğan

Introduction

For the last decade, the number of empirical studies, which reveal the strategic importance of corporate social responsibility activities for the tourism and hospitality industry, is increasing. To put forward the importance of these practices for enterprises, the first studies conducted mostly relate to financial performance (He *et al.*, 2019). Aguinis and Glavas (2012) describe these studies as macro-CSR research. However, recently, there have been increasing studies called micro-CSR research that investigate stakeholders' CSR perceptions and their effect on their attitudes and behaviours. Among these stakeholders, mostly customers (Kim *et al.*, 2017; Huang and Cheng, 2016), current employees (Kim *et al.*, 2018; Gürlek and Tuna, 2019; He *et al.*, 2019), prospective employees (Boğan and Dedeoğlu, 2019) and local people (Gursoy *et al.*, 2019) are examined. The current study is micro-CSR research and examines current employees returns to CSR practices. Employees' returns on CSR practices investigated in tourism and hospitality sub-sectors namely hotel (Park and Levy, 2014), casino (Youn *et al.*, 2018), travel agency (Park *et al.*, 2018), airline company (Ilkhanizadeh and Karatepe 2017). In these sectors, large and luxury enterprises were examined, and small enterprises were not examined sufficiently (Jenkins, 2006; Kim *et al.*, 2017; Serra-Cantallops *et al.*, 2018; Asante Boadi *et al.*, 2019). As the reasons for large-scale enterprises are examined, it is shown that luxury and large-scale hotels have more social responsibility activities than others and higher levels of awareness about CSR (Nyahunzvi, 2013). However, regardless of scale, each entity has social and environmental responsibilities in the region where it operates. Besides, a large part of the tourism sector is composed of small- and medium-scale enterprises. Therefore, it is essential to examine CSR activities in these enterprises. The fact that these enterprises, which constitute a large part of the sector, are not examined adequately does not mean that these enterprises do not exhibit social and environmental responsibility

DOI: 10.4324/9780429281228-4

practices (Lee and Kim, 2013). Recently, social, economic, and environmental responsibility practices have become more obvious and important for small and medium accommodation enterprises (Garay and Font, 2012). Yet, the most common form of responsibility practice is philanthropy (Jenkins, 2006). According to Rhou and Singal (2020) "research on CSR towards communities, such as charitable giving ..., appears to be one of the less-studied themes in the current hospitality literature" (p. 5). Some small-scaled hospitality companies operating in Turkey, as a reflection of religious values the manager or owner has, deliver Ramadan packages to employees and communities in need. However as stated by Jenkins (2006: 246) they are unaware that their actions could be described as CSR practices. This is because they have less knowledge about the strategic importance of CSR practices in small service firms. Ramadan packages contain pulses such as haricot bean, chickpea, lentil, oil, etc. By delivering these packages to employees and communities, small-scaled hospitality companies exhibit corporate citizenship exemplary. In this study, the contribution of this initiative to employees' CSR perceptions and the effect of these perceptions on their trust in the organization and organizational citizenship behaviour are discussed.

Literature Review and Hypothesis Development

This study discusses the effect of delivering Ramadan packages to people in need on employees' CSR perceptions. It also discusses the effect of employees' CSR perceptions on organizational citizenship behaviour through the mediation of trust in the organization. Lastly, the role of employees perceived corporate sincerity as a moderator on the relationship between Ramadan packages and CSR perception discussed.

Corporate Social Responsibility in Small-scaled Hospitality Companies

The concept of corporate social responsibility is of great interest to both academics and practitioners. CSR is an important concept that emphasizes that businesses should take into consideration not only their own economic interests but also social interests (McGuire, 1963). In the literature, although it is used synonymously with names such as corporate governance, corporate citizenship, corporate giving, and corporate responsibility (Kim *et al.*, 2017), it can be said that the concept of CSR is mostly used in the literature. Currently, in addition to the pressure exerted by the state and stakeholders on businesses, many enterprises are involved in social and environmental initiatives regardless of their scale, as empirical studies have contributed both to the operational financial performance of the CSR (Rodríguez and del Mar Armas Cruz 2007) and

58   Erhan Boğan

to positive feedback from stakeholders (Aguilera *et al.*, 2007). Businesses aim to establish a good relationship with their stakeholders by announcing these initiatives to their stakeholders through different channels (Holcomb *et al.*, 2007; de Grosbois, 2012).

The concept of CSR is not a new concept in the tourism and hospitality industry. Previously, however, it was often identified with environmental initiatives of hotels (Sheldon and Park, 2011). In other words, CSR activities in the tourism sector focused on environmental initiatives (energy saving, water saving, etc.) which are one of the three main components of sustainability (Garay and Font, 2012). In recent years, however, economic, and social initiatives, two other important components of sustainability, have come to the forefront (Gursoy *et al.*, 2019). When it comes to small-scale hotels, it is possible to say that social and environmental initiatives are very limited. This is mainly due to factors such as low level of awareness of management, financial constraints, lack of learning, and lack of knowledge that the activity is social responsibility (Farmaki, 2019; Fassin *et al.*, 2011; November 2009; Merwe and Wöcke, 2007; Jenkins, 2006). In small-scale hotels, the business owner is also the manager and basically focuses on solving everyday problems. Communication and relations with stakeholders are informal and often mimic or be influenced by businesses operating in the market. The decision-making process is dominated by an amateur understanding of the business owner's desire or view of life rather than a professional one (Fassin *et al.*, 2011; Murillo and Lozano, 2006).

It is now widely accepted that social responsibility practices are not only good for the community but also for companies involved (Maignan and Ferrell, 2003; Njite *et al.*, 2011; Gursoy *et al.*, 2019). This reality applies not only to large or luxury businesses, but also to small businesses. However, there are only a few studies about CSR practices in small-scaled hospitality companies (Thomas *et al.*, 2011). According to the findings of Njite *et al.* (2011), managers of small and independent hotels indicated that social responsibility practices may not immediately raise profitability in the short run, however, it is vital for companies' survival and competition in long run. Contrary to studies (Kang *et al.*, 2010; Lee *et al.*, 2013) that revealed mixed results regarding the impact of CSR on financial performance, Garay and Font (2012) found that small and medium-sized hotels' social, environmental, and economic responsible practices improve financial performance. Singal (2014) found that family firms in the hospitality and tourism industry invest more in CSR practices compared to nonfamily firms. According to her, CSR practices could help family firms to improve their financial performance. Alonso-Almeida *et al.* (2018) found that social responsibility practices implemented by small service firms increase firms' financial performance and market success factors as company image, customer- and employee satisfaction in Spain (Figure 3.1).

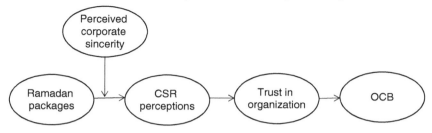

Figure 3.1 Conceptual Model.

Ramadan Packages and CSR Perceptions

There are different views or approaches to the definition of the concept of corporate social responsibility, which is a commodity structure, and what it contains (Rupp and Mallory, 2015). Researchers are hesitant to consider within the concept of social responsibility (e.g. providing a safe work environment, training for their employees) that are legally or normatively responsible for undertaking against their stakeholders (e.g. employees). Because these initiatives are not the manifestation of the expression "voluntary initiatives beyond legal regulations" in the definition of CSR. These initiatives should be considered under different concepts (e.g. human resource management) rather than CSR (Rupp and Mallory 2015). In the present study, the definition made by the Commissions of European Communities (EC) was accepted as the definition of Commission of the European Communities (2001) defined CSR as "a concept whereby companies integrate social and environmental concerns in their business operations and in their interaction with their stakeholders on a voluntary basis" which is one of the most accepted definitions of CSR (Dahlsrud, 2008). This definition includes companies' philanthropic initiatives as delivering Ramadan Packages to people in need.

In Ramadan, which is one of the holy months for Muslim people, Ramadan packages that include different supplies (tea, sugar, flour, oil, rice, bulgur, pasta, etc.) are delivered to poor or needy families. The content of this package is directly proportional to the generosity of the charitable person. Many business owners from different sectors need to make this assistance to employees or families in Turkey. In the tourism sector, this type of assistance is often carried out in small-scale family businesses, where the owner is also responsible for the business management. Mostly, it is carried out with religious or moral values owned by the business owner. Muslims fast in the month of Ramadan. The fasting is one of the conditions of Islam. In social life, people are created in different ways at the point of livelihood. Based on this contrast, God invites the rich to help the people in need. The rich can feel the pitiful suffering and hunger of the needy people in full while fasting or fasting

60   *Erhan Boğan*

month. According to Islamic belief, if there is no obligation to starve, one cannot make the bestowal and help that he is obliged by help through compassion; if he does, it will not be complete. Because he does not feel the real situation in his own self. At this point, especially during Ramadan, the assistance they provide to needy employees or non-business individuals by creating a Ramadan package may strengthen the employees' perception of corporate social responsibility. Based on this, the following hypothesis can be established.

H1. Delivering Ramadan packages to those people in need fosters employees' CSR perception.

CSR Perceptions and Trust in Organization

Among the studies investigating the returns of employees to CSR, trust in an organization is one of the least researched concepts (Farooq *et al.*, 2013). When the situation comes in the tourism and hospitality industry, the deficiency becomes more pronounced. Only a few studies examined the impact of employees' CSR perceptions on trust in organisation in hospitality context (Boğan and Dedeoğlu, 2019; Su and Swanson, 2019; Lee *et al.*, 2013; Lee *et al.*, 2012). Social exchange theory is one of the most cited theory while examining the relation between CSR perception and employees' trust in organisation (Boğan and Dedeoğlu, 2019; Farooq *et al.*, 2013). One of the most fundamental principles of social exchange theory is the rule of reciprocity, which is the basis of all exchanges. There are two forms of exchange that could explain the relationship between concepts as direct (restricted) and generalized exchange. In direct exchange, there are two parties that provide benefits to each other. However, in the generalized exchange, there are at least three parties. Each party provides, and eventually receives benefits, but not to and from the same party (Cropanzano and Mitchell, 2005; Molm *et al.*, 2007; Farooq *et al.*, 2013). Hotel managements' social responsibility practices towards employees and outside stakeholders (e.g. community) can be evaluated under both direct and generalized exchange. Specifically, when hotel fulfills responsibilities to employees beyond legal and economic dimensions (such as delivering Ramadan packages), employees give back as good as they get. Based on deontic justice theory (Cropanzano *et al.*, 2003), employees demand fair behaviours from companies not only for themselves but also for society at large. Hotels managements' social responsibility practices towards the community can be evaluated as responding to this demand. That means, hotel employees could indirectly reciprocate actions that the hotel takes for the welfare of the community.

In addition to the theoretical background as above mentioned, there are some publications that found a positive impact of social responsibility perceptions on trust in organisation, specifically in hotels. Based on the theoretical baseline and in replication of findings of previous studies (Boğan and Dedeoğlu, 2019; Su and Swanson, 2019; Lee *et al.*, 2013; Lee *et al.*, 2012), we propose the following hypothesis:

H2. Hotel employees' CSR perceptions positively impact their trust in organisation.

Trust in Organization and Organizational Citizenship Behavior

Organizational citizenship behaviour is defined as "individual behaviour that is discretionary, not directly or explicitly recognized by the formal reward system, and that in the aggregate promotes the effective functioning of the organization" (Organ, 1988: 4). In this chapter, we formulate that small-scaled hospitality company employees' trust in organisation positively affect their desire to display citizenship behaviours as tolerating imperfect situations, helping coworkers to solve the problems, going beyond minimum requirements through hard work. Employees' positive organizational behaviours such as OCB are not only important to achieving business goals but also important to creating a competitive advantage for hospitality companies (Karatepe and Sokmen, 2006) since this industry places more emphasis on service-oriented behaviour (Morrison, 1996). The empirical evidence has shown that organizational trust is an important driver of OCB (Yoon, Jang, and Lee, 2016; Wat and Shaffer, 2005; Podsakoff *et al.*, 1990). However, most of these studies sample from luxury or upscale companies. Only a few studies examined the relationship among these concepts specifically in small-scale hospitality companies. Therefore, we propose that:

H3. Employees' trust in organisation positively impacting organizational citizenship behaviour.

The Mediating Effect of Trust in Organization

Trust in the organization is an underlying mechanism through which employees' CSR perception affects organizational citizenship behaviour. The effect of CSR perception of tourism and hospitality industry employees on organizational citizenship behaviour was investigated in some studies directly (Kim *et al.*, 2017) and in others by mediating variables (indirectly) (Raub and Blunschi, 2014; Fu *et al.*, 2014; Ilkhanizadeh and Karatepe, 2017; He, Zhang, and Morrison, 2019). Most of these studies found a positive effect of CSR on organizational citizenship behaviour.

62 *Erhan Boğan*

In positive relationship between employee CSR perceptions and organizational citizenship behaviour in hospitality industry, mostly work engagement (Ilkhanizadeh and Karatepe, 2017), organizational identification (He, Zhang, and Morrison, 2019; Fu, Ye, and Law, 2014), affective commitment (Fu, Ye, and Law, 2014), task significance (Raub and Blunschi, 2014) is explored as mediators. Only few studies examined the role of employees' trust in organisation as a mediator (Yoon, Jang, and Lee, 2016; Yu and Choi, 2014).

Trust has often been used as a mediating variable in marketing and management literature. One of the most decisive factors of positive organizational outcomes is trust. Perhaps the most important factor in providing positive feedback to the business by the charitable activities carried out to benefit the society and its employees outside the company's own field of activity is perhaps how much trust the stakeholders have in the enterprise (Yoon, Jang, and Lee, 2016). Through these initiatives, the entity sends signals to its internal and external stakeholders about its ethical and moral values. As these philanthropic initiatives are made not only for the external stakeholders of the enterprise but also for internal stakeholders, their perception of integrity is strengthened and their credibility increases (McShane and Cunningham, 2012). Therefore, the trust of the stakeholders is gained. In addition, the enterprise transmits messages to stakeholders about its helpful identity through these initiatives. It can be expected that CSR activities can help to achieve trust in the organization since benevolence and integrity are two components of trustworthiness (Mayer *et al.*, 1995).

The role of organizational trust in leading positive organizational behaviours such as organizational citizenship behaviour (Kannan-Narasimhan and Lawrence, 2012), altruism (Hon and Lu, 2010), job performance (Palanski and Yammarino, 2011) is well documented in previous studies. Since employees' trust in the organization is a consequence of CSR perception and one of the predictors of organizational citizenship behaviour, we formulated the following hypothesis:

H4. Trust in the organization at least partially mediates the relationship between employees' CSR perception and OCB.

The Moderating Role of Perceived Corporate Sincerity

The main motivations that lead hospitality companies to implement economic, social and environmental practices that provide benefits both for the organization and society at large have been investigated by a number of researchers (Merwe and Wöcke, 2007; Huimin and Ryan, 2011; Garay and Font, 2012; Sandve and Øgaard, 2014). These practices are mostly implemented with altruistic reasons, strategic/economic reasons, gain legitimation from stakeholders, manager/owner's personal/ ethical values, and legislative regulations. Although the environmental initiatives undertaken by hospitality businesses are mostly aimed at saving costs in the long term and maintaining a competitive position, it is possible to say those social enterprises put in place with altruistic or intrinsic motives (Garay and Font, 2012; Jenkins, 2006). Although enterprises display social responsibility with different motives, one of the factors that enable these enterprises to make positive feedback to the enterprise is the judgments made by the stakeholders to these initiatives. In other words, they are the implications of how these initiatives are realized (Brown *et al.*, 2006; Cha *et al.*, 2016). According to attribution theory (Kelley and Michela, 1980), employees observe both the internal and external behaviours/activities of the entity and make judgments about the possible causes of the activities. Because people are more interested in why they do it than what others do (Gilbert and Malone, 1995). The opinions and interpretations of the employees significantly affect their attitudes and behaviours towards the company. Nowadays, stakeholders are sceptical about the enterprises that carry out social responsibility activities. The use of these activities as a means of advertising may strengthen these doubts, which may lead to the idea that these activities are not realistic or sincere (Lange and Washburn, 2012; Zhang, Yang, and Zheng, 2018). Therefore, it can be expected that employees 'perception of the company's sincerity will have a moderate effect on the strengthening of employees' social responsibility perception by the Ramadan package distributed by hotels. At present, the hotel's benevolent activity during Ramadan, the holy month for Muslims, may prove that this activity was carried out with moral or religious values, that is, with sincere intent. Based on these explanations, we propose that;

H5. Perceived corporate sincerity amplifies the effect of Ramadan packages on employees' CSR perception.

Main Contributions

In this chapter, we build a comprehensive theoretical model on small-scaled hotel employees' responses to Ramadan packages as CSR practices. This theoretical model provides some unique contributions to existing hospitality literature. First, in contrast to the previous studies, a specific responsible initiative, known as the Ramadan package, carried out by small-scale hotels, was highlighted in this study. The impact of this responsible activity on employees' perception of CSR was discussed. Unlike studies that directly examine employee attitudes and behaviours of CSR activities, the present study first dealt with one of the components affecting CSR perception specifically in small-scale hotels. Understanding

64 Erhan Boğan

of antecedents shaping employees' CSR perceptions will, therefore, allow for more focused hypothesis testing in future research. Second, we argue and explain the role of employees perceived corporate sincerity regarding CSR practices as one of the key variables that amplify the effect of a philanthropic practice on employees' CSR perception. Although we have recently coincided studies that examine employees' intrinsic-CSR attribution as a boundary condition for the positive effect of CSR on employee outcomes, only a few studies examined the boundary condition in hospitality context, specifically small-scaled hotels. By arguing and explaining employees perceived corporate sincerity, this study focused filling this literature gap in hospitality context. Third, although in previous paper it was emphasized to discovering underlying mechanism that links CSR to employee attitudes and behaviours, only few studies focused to fill this gap (Aguinis and Glavas, 2012; Ilkhanizadeh and Karatepe, 2017). Accordingly, we discuss trust in organisation as the underlying mechanism through which CSR perception is linked to small-scaled hotel employees' organizational citizenship behaviour. Lastly, we address a recent call focusing CSR implementation and impacts in small-scale hotels and the Mediterranean region (Serra-Cantallops *et al.*, 2018).

Conclusion

This chapter proposes a theoretical model explaining how a specific socially responsible behaviour implemented by small-scaled hotels can contribute to employees' CSR perception which in turn leads to positive employee outcomes. We highlight that employees' corporate sincerity perception may help to foster the effect of delivering Ramadan packages to people in need on CSR perception. We also highlight that employees' CSR perceptions can foster their organizational citizenship behaviour through trust in their organization. However, all these proposed hypotheses need an empirical test that can be conducted at the individual level of analysis.

References

Aguilera, R.V. *et al.* (2007) 'Putting the S back in corporate social responsibility: A multilevel theory of social change in organizations', *Academy of Management Review*, 3(3), pp. 836–863.

Aguinis, H. and Glavas, A. (2012) 'What we know and don't know about corporate social responsibility a review and research agenda', *Journal of Management*, 38(4), pp. 932–968.

Alonso-Almeida, M.D.M. *et al.* (2018) 'Sustainability in small tourist businesses: the link between initiatives and performance', *Current Issues in Tourism*, 21(1), pp. 1–20.

Asante Boadi, E. *et al.* (2019) 'Employees' perception of corporate social responsibility (CSR) and its effects on internal outcomes', *The Service Industries Journal*, 40, pp. 1–23.

Boğan, E. and Dedeoğlu, B.B. (2017) The link between perceived corporate social responsibility, commitment to tourism industry and willingness to recommend the organization, In 7th Advances in Hospitality and Tourism Marketing and Management Conference (AHTMM), pp. 120–134, Famagusta, North Cyprus.

Boğan, E. and Dedeoğlu, B.B. (2019) 'The effects of hotel employees' CSR perceptions on trust in organization', *Journal of Hospitality and Tourism Insights*. November 5th 2012. 10.1108/JHTI-12-2018-0089.

Brown, T.J. *et al.* (2006) 'Identity, intended image, construed image, and reputation: An interdisciplinary framework and suggested terminology', *Journal of the Academy of Marketing Science*, 34(2), pp. 99–106.

Cha, M.K., Yi, Y., and Bagozzi, R.P. (2016) 'Effects of customer participation in corporate social responsibility (CSR) programs on the CSR-brand fit and brand loyalty', *Cornell Hospitality Quarterly*, 57(3), pp. 235–249.

Commission of the European Communities (2001) Promoting a European Framework for Corporate Social Responsibilities, COM (2001) 366 final, Brussels.

Cropanzano, R. and Mitchell, M.S. (2005) 'Social exchange theory: An interdisciplinary review', *Journal of Management*, 31(6), pp. 874–900.

Cropanzano, R., Goldman, B., and Folger, R. (2003) 'Deontic justice: The role of moral principles in workplace fairness', *Journal of Organizational Behavior*, 24(8), pp. 1019–1024.

Dahlsrud, A. (2008) 'How corporate social responsibility is defined: an analysis of 37 definitions', *Corporate Social Responsibility and Environmental Management*, 15(1), pp. 1–13.

de Grosbois, D. (2012) 'Corporate social responsibility reporting by the global hotel industry: Commitment, initiatives and performance', *International Journal of Hospitality Management*, 31(3), pp. 896–905.

Farmaki, A. (2019) 'Corporate social responsibility in hotels: a stakeholder approach', *International Journal of Contemporary Hospitality Management*, 31(6), pp. 2297–2320.

Farooq O., Merunka D., and Valette-Florence P. (2013) 'Employees' response to corporate social responsibility: An application of a nonlinear mixture REBUS approach'. In Abdi H., Chin W., Esposito Vinzi V., Russolillo G., Trinchera L. (eds.), *New perspectives in partial least squares and related methods. Springer Proceedings in Mathematics & Statistics*. New York, NY: Springer, Vol 56.

Fassin, Y., Van Rossem, A., and Buelens, M. (2011) 'Small-business owner-managers' perceptions of business ethics and CSR-related concepts', *Journal of Business ethics*, 98(3), pp. 425–453.

Fu, H., Ye, B.H., and Law, R. (2014) 'You do well and I do well? The behavioral consequences of corporate social responsibility', *International Journal of Hospitality Management*, 40, pp. 62–70.

Garay, L., and Font, X. (2012) 'Doing good to do well? Corporate social responsibility reasons, practices and impacts in small and medium accommodation enterprises', *International Journal of Hospitality Management*, 31(2), pp. 329–337.

Gilbert, D.T. and Malone, P.S. (1995) 'The correspondence bias', *Psychological Bulletin*, 117(1), pp. 21–38.

Gursoy, D. *et al.* (2019) 'Residents' perceptions of hotels' corporate social responsibility initiatives and its impact on residents' sentiments to community and support for additional tourism development', *Journal of Hospitality and Tourism Management*, 39, pp. 117–128.

66 *Erhan Boğan*

Gürlek, M. and Tuna, M. (2019) 'Corporate social responsibility and work engagement: Evidence from the hotel industry', *Tourism Management Perspectives*, 31, pp. 195–208.

He, J., Zhang, H., and Morrison, A.M. (2019) 'The impacts of corporate social responsibility on organization citizenship behavior and task performance in hospitality: A sequential mediation model', *International Journal of Contemporary Hospitality Management*, 31(6), pp. 2582–2598.

Holcomb, J.L., Upchurch, R.S., and Okumus, F. (2007) 'Corporate social responsibility: what are top hotel companies reporting?', *International Journal of contemporary Hospitality Management*, 19(6), pp. 461–475.

Hon, A.H. and Lu, L. (2010) 'The mediating role of trust between expatriate procedural justice and employee outcomes in Chinese hotel industry', *International Journal of Hospitality Management*, 29(4), pp. 669–676.

Huang, M.H. and Cheng, Z.H. (2016) 'Strategies to enhance consumers' identification with a service firm', *Journal of Services Marketing*, 30(4), pp. 449–461.

Huimin, G. and Ryan, C. (2011) 'Ethics and corporate social responsibility–An analysis of the views of Chinese hotel managers', *International Journal of Hospitality Management*, 30(4), pp. 875–885.

Ilkhanizadeh, S. and Karatepe, O.M. (2017) 'An examination of the consequences of corporate social responsibility in the airline industry: Work engagement, career satisfaction, and voice behavior', *Journal of Air Transport Management*, 59, pp. 8–17.

Jenkins, H. (2006) 'Small business champions for corporate social responsibility', *Journal of Business Ethics*, 67(3), pp. 241–256.

Kang, K.H., Lee, S., and Huh, C. (2010) 'Impacts of positive and negative corporate social responsibility activities on company performance in the hospitality industry', *International Journal of Hospitality Management*, 29(1), pp. 72–82.

Kannan-Narasimhan, R. and Lawrence, B.S. (2012) 'Behavioral integrity: How leader referents and trust matter to workplace outcomes', *Journal of Business Ethics*, 111(2), pp. 165–178.

Karatepe, O.M. and Sokmen, A. (2006) 'The effects of work role and family role variables on psychological and behavioral outcomes of frontline employees', *Tourism Management*, 27(2), pp. 255–268.

Kasim, A. (2009) 'Managerial attitudes towards environmental management among small and medium hotels in Kuala Lumpur', *Journal of Sustainable Tourism*, 17 (6), pp. 709–725.

Kelley, H.H. and Michela, J.L. (1980) 'Attribution theory and research', *Annual Review of Psychology*, 31(1), pp. 457–501.

Kim, H.L. *et al.* (2017) 'An examination of the links between corporate social responsibility (CSR) and its internal consequences', *International Journal of Hospitality Management*, 61, pp. 26–34.

Kim, H. *et al.* (2018) 'The effects of corporate social responsibility (CSR) on employee well-being in the hospitality industry', *International Journal of Contemporary Hospitality Management*, 30 (3), pp. 1584–1600.

Kim, J.S. *et al.* (2017) 'The impact of four CSR dimensions on a gaming company's image and customers' revisit intentions', *International Journal of Hospitality Management*, 61, pp. 73–81.

Corporate Social Responsibility Practice   67

Lange, D., and Washburn, N.T. (2012) 'Understanding attributions of corporate social irresponsibility', *Academy of Management Review*, 37(2), pp. 300–326.

Lee, C.K. *et al.* (2013) 'The impact of CSR on casino employees' organizational trust, job satisfaction, and customer orientation: An empirical examination of responsible gambling strategies', *International Journal of Hospitality Management*, 33, pp. 406–415.

Lee, M. and Kim, W. (2013) 'The effect of perceived corporate social responsibility on hotel employee's attitude and behavior toward the organization', *International Journal of Tourism Sciences*, 13(3), pp. 51–74.

Lee, S., Singal, M., and Kang, K.H. (2013) 'The corporate social responsibility–financial performance link in the US restaurant industry: do economic conditions matter?', *International Journal of Hospitality Management*, 32, pp. 2–10.

Lee, Y.K. *et al.* (2012) 'The impact of CSR on relationship quality and relationship outcomes: A perspective of service employees', *International Journal of Hospitality Management*, 31(3), pp. 745–756.

Maignan, I. and Ferrell, O.C. (2003) 'Nature of corporate responsibilities: Perspectives from American, French, and German consumers', *Journal of Business Research*, 56: pp. 55–67.

McGuire, J.W. (1963) *Business and society*. New York: McGraw-Hill.

McShane, L. and Cunningham, P. (2012) 'To thine own self be true? Employees' judgments of the authenticity of their organization's corporate social responsibility program', *Journal of business ethics*, 108(1), pp. 81–100.

Mayer, R.C., Davis, J.H., and Schoorman, F.D. (1995) 'An integrative model of organizational trust', *Academy of Management Review*, 20(3), pp. 709–734.

Merwe, M. and Wöcke, A. (2007) 'An investigation into responsible tourism practices in the South African hotel industry', *South African Journal of Business Management*, 38(2), pp. 1–15.

Molm, L.D., Collett, J.L., and Schaefer, D.R. (2007) 'Building solidarity through generalized exchange: A theory of reciprocity', *American Journal of Sociology*, 113(1), pp. 205–242.

Morrison, E.W. (1996) 'Organizational citizenship behavior as a critical link between HRM practices and service quality', *Human Resource Management*, 35(4), pp. 493–512.

Murillo, D. and Lozano, J.M. (2006) 'SMEs and CSR: An approach to CSR in their own words', *Journal of Business Ethics*, 67(3), pp. 227–240.

Njite, D., Hancer, M., and Slevitch, L. (2011) 'Exploring corporate social responsibility: A managers' perspective on how and why small independent hotels engage with their communities', *Journal of Quality Assurance in Hospitality & Tourism*, 12(3), pp. 177–201.

Nyahunzvi, K.D. (2013) 'CSR reporting among Zimbabwe's hotel groups: a content analysis', *International Journal of Contemporary Hospitality Management*, 25(4), pp. 595–613.

Organ, D.W. (1988) *Organizational citizenship behavior: The good soldier syndrome*. Lexington, MA: Lexington Books.

Palanski, M.E. and Yammarino, F.J. (2011) 'Impact of behavioral integrity on follower job performance: A three-study examination', *The Leadership Quarterly*, 22 (4), pp. 765–786.

68 Erhan Boğan

Park, S.Y. and Levy, S.E. (2014) 'Corporate social responsibility: perspectives of hotel frontline employees', *International Journal of Contemporary Hospitality Management*, 26(3), pp. 332–348.

Park, S.Y., Lee, C.K., and Kim, H. (2018) 'The influence of corporate social responsibility on travel company employees', *International Journal of Contemporary Hospitality Management*, 30(1), pp. 178–196.

Podsakoff, P.M. *et al.* (1990) 'Transformational leader behaviors and their effects on followers' trust in leader, satisfaction, and organizational citizenship behaviors', *The leadership Quarterly*, 1(2), pp. 107–142.

Raub, S., and Blunschi, S. (2014) 'The power of meaningful work: How awareness of CSR initiatives fosters task significance and positive work outcomes in service employees', *Cornell Hospitality Quarterly*, 55(1), pp. 10–18.

Rhou, Y. and Singal, M. (2020) 'A review of the business case for CSR in the hospitality industry', *International Journal of Hospitality Management*, 84, pp. 102–334. 10.1016/j.ijhm.2019.102330.

Rodríguez, F.J.G. and del Mar Armas Cruz, Y. (2007) 'Relation between social-environmental responsibility and performance in hotel firms', *International Journal of Hospitality Management*, 26(4), pp. 824–839.

Rupp, D.E. and Mallory, D.B. (2015) 'Corporate social responsibility: Psychological, person-centric, and progressing', *Annu. Rev. Organ. Psychol. Organ. Behav.*, 2(1), pp. 211–236.

Sandve, A. and Øgaard, T. (2014) 'Exploring the interaction between perceived ethical obligation and subjective norms, and their influence on CSR-related choices', *Tourism Management*, 42, pp. 177–180.

Serra-Cantallops, A. *et al.* (2018) 'Progress in research on CSR and the hotel industry (2006-2015)', *Cornell Hospitality Quarterly*, 5 (1), pp. 15–38.

Sheldon, P.J. and Park, S.Y. (2011) 'An exploratory study of corporate social responsibility in the US travel industry', *Journal of Travel Research*, 50(4), pp. 392–407.

Singal, M. (2014) 'Corporate social responsibility in the hospitality and tourism industry: do family control and financial condition matter?', *International Journal of Hospitality Management*, 36, pp. 81–89.

Su, L. and Swanson, S.R. (2019) 'Perceived corporate social responsibility's impact on the well-being and supportive green behaviors of hotel employees: The mediating role of the employee-corporate relationship', *Tourism Management*, 72, pp. 437–450.

Thomas, R., Shaw, G., and Page, S.J. (2011) 'Understanding small firms in tourism: A perspective on research trends and challenges', *Tourism Management*, 32(5), pp. 963–976.

Wat, D. and Shaffer, M.A. (2005) 'Equity and relationship quality influences on organizational citizenship behaviors: The mediating role of trust in the supervisor and empowerment', *Personnel review*, 34(4), pp. 406–422.

Yoon, D., Jang, J., and Lee, J. (2016) 'Environmental management strategy and organizational citizenship behaviors in the hotel industry: The mediating role of organizational trust and commitment', *International Journal of Contemporary Hospitality Management*, 28(8), pp. 1577–1597.

Youn, H., Lee, K., and Lee, S. (2018) 'Effects of corporate social responsibility on employees in the casino industry', *Tourism Management*, 68, pp. 328–335.

Yu, Y. and Choi, Y. (2014) 'Corporate social responsibility and firm performance through the mediating effect of organizational trust in Chinese firms', *Chinese Management Studies*, 8(4), pp. 577–592.

Zhang, L., Yang, W., and Zheng, X. (2018) 'Corporate social responsibility: the effect of need-for-status and fluency on consumers' attitudes', *International Journal of Contemporary Hospitality Management*, 30(3), pp. 1492–1507.

4 Antecedents and Influences of Corporate Citizenship: Case Study of a Finnish Family Firm

Ahmad Arslan,
Pia Hurmelinna-Laukkanen,
Lauri Haapanen, and
Dr Deborah Callaghan

Introduction

Corporate citizenship is most commonly defined as "the extent to which businesses meet the economic, legal, ethical and discretionary responsibilities imposed on them by stakeholders" (Maignan and Ferrell, 2000: 284). Firms that embrace corporate citizenship are typically characterized by having a more strategic (long term) orientation, complemented by a willingness to contribute to wider society (Crane and Matten, 2016). In general, corporate citizenship has been noted to result in increased support for the firm from relevant stakeholders (e.g. Crane and Matten, 2016) and is also shown to result in heightened levels of employee engagement (e.g. Glavas and Piderit, 2009) and positive performance effects.

Many prior studies have argued that family-owned firms are often better corporate citizens compared to their corporate counterparts (e.g. Deephouse and Jaskiewicz, 2013; Campopiano and De Massis, 2015; Binz *et al.*, 2017). One of the reasons for this is the inclination of family firms to view business from a long-term perspective rather than to place emphasis on short-term financial gains, which often comes at the cost of others or resources. The founders of family firms often emphasize their legacy (Hammond *et al.*, 2016) which has been highlighted to play a key role in shaping the strategy, structure, and long-term focus of such firms (e.g. Kelly *et al.*, 2000). In many cases, family firms and their founders have intergenerational history, or desire to create and own one (e.g. Neubauer and Lank, 2016). This long-term perspective can act as a powerful motivator for corporate citizenship and can lead these firms to go beyond short-term monetary gains as the only measure of success. It also pushes them towards a socioemotional wealth model (Berrone *et al.*, 2012). In sum, prior literature has referred to issues like non-financial wealth, social advancement, status in society, and other reputational advantages as important elements for family firms (Binz *et al.*, 2017). In fact, it has been suggested that the reputational advantage that stems

DOI: 10.4324/9780429281228-5

Antecedents of Corporate Citizenship   71

from corporate citizenship behaviour is the main source of competitiveness for family firms (Deephouse and Jaskiewicz, 2013; Campopiano and De Massis, 2015; Binz *et al.*, 2017).

This brings us to the focus of this study. Block and Wagner (2014: 477) suggest that the "literature pertaining to CSR (corporate social responsibility) in family firms can be categorized as: (1) empirical papers analysing CSR performance in family firms and (2) papers seeking to explain the different motives of family firms for pursuing non-family stakeholder-oriented goals." Our view is somewhat different, as we look at both drivers and influences for corporate citizenship in family firms. In particular, we aim to increase understanding of the interplay reputational advantage, socioemotional wealth, founder's experiences and vision, and intergenerational aspirations, with corporate citizenship behaviour in family firms. We undertake an exploratory case study of a family-owned firm in Nordic context (in Finland), that operates in a very competitive medical supplies service sector. The main client base of the case firm includes both public sector organisations, including hospitals and health care centres, and private sector health care centres and other private organisations. We are particularly interested in studying how corporate citizenship in the case firm interrelates with reputational advantage as well as with the founder's vision and experience. We also focus on the socioemotional wealth associated with reputational advantage for family firms and examine how it plays a role in this specific context (cf., e.g. Berrone *et al.*, 2012; Gomez-Mejia *et al.*, 2011). Furthermore, the current chapter attempts to analyse the influences of corporate citizenship on customer behaviour by focusing on potential differences between public and private sector customers of case firm. By doing so, we attempt to fill a gap in existing literature, as customer segmentation in the above-mentioned categories has not been specifically addressed in the context of corporate citizenship by family firms. Finally, as the case firm operates in the medical supplies service sector, we believe that it offers a very good empirical setting to analyse factors such as reputational advantage, founder's vision and experience on corporate citizenship in the context of the family firm. In combination, these elements bring new insight into the discussion on corporate citizenship and family firms, narrowing the existing gaps in the field.

The structure of the chapter is as follows. The next section offers a theoretical overview, where key themes relevant to the topic are conceptually addressed. This is followed by a presentation of the case study and findings. The chapter concludes with a discussion of the implications, limitations and future research directions.

Theoretical Overview

Corporate citizenship refers to firms dealing specifically with 'social' aspects of corporate responsibility (Waddock and Smith, 2000). Corporate

72   Arslan et al.

citizenship consists of different actions including both commercial and philanthropic activities with the goals of ensuring profitability while at the same time, going beyond mere compliance with minimum legal requirements. This involves engaging in ethical behaviour resulting in benefits for the greater community (Matten *et al.*, 2003). Many businesses are increasingly engaging in corporate citizenship associated activities due to the positive reputational advantages that are associated with it (Gardberg and Fombrun, 2006; Saeed and Arshad, 2012; Campopiano and De Massis, 2015; Binz *et al.*, 2017) despite contradictory evidence of the potential financial or organisational benefits yielded through long-term reputational advantage (e.g. Galbreath, 2006; Halme and Laurila, 2009; Crane and Matten, 2016).

In prior research, family firms are established to be different from non-family firms in a variety of ways (Gudmundson, Hartman, and Tower, 1999; Zahra *et al.*, 2004; De Massis *et al.*, 2015), and this also extends to how they engage in corporate citizenship. Although it has been noted that "family firms can be responsible and irresponsible regarding CSR at the same time" (Block and Wagner, 2014: 475), there are certain aspects of family firms that can potentially foster corporate citizenship behaviour. These aspects have been addressed in existing literature, covering, for example, relative lack of shareholder pressure for profit maximisation in the short term (Carney *et al.*, 2015; Miller *et al.*, 2018), and founder's vision, family values, and intergenerational aspirations (e.g. Jaskiewicz, Combs, and Rau, 2015; Baschieri *et al.*, 2017). Relatedly, it has been established that family firms tend to take a long-term perspective on financial outcomes and that they have a higher commitment to their local communities (Aronoff and Ward, 2016; Baschieri *et al.*, 2017). We offer a brief theoretical discussion on each of these related but distinctive aspects in the following sections.

Limited Shareholder Pressure in Family Firms

Prior literature has indicated that shareholder pressure for short term gains and profit maximisation can lead to profit-centric and short-term behaviour in certain listed firms (e.g. Crane and Matten, 2016; Gavana *et al.*, 2017). As family firms hold the desire to leave a healthy legacy to future generations, this often results in them being more resistant to actions that may harm their links with the broader community. (e.g. Cruz *et al.*, 2014; Aronoff and Ward, 2016). Moreover, it has been argued that this relatively closer relationship with the broader community sometimes results in family firms taking a more active stance in corporate citizenship activities because they see the survival and long-term viability of the family firm to be connected to the betterment of the local community (Crane and Matten, 2016; Baschieri *et al.*, 2017). While it is not always family firms that take upon such endeavours as charitable giving,

Antecedents of Corporate Citizenship 73

donations to local institutions, housing support or subsistence markets (see Block and Wagner, 2014), it is this close relationship with the community that generally enables family firms to build social capital (e.g. Arregle *et al.*, 2007; Le Breton-Miller *et al.*, 2015 and Miller *et al.*, 2018). Family firms are found to be relatively more enlightened, favouring long-term oriented strategies that foster lasting relationships with customers and the wider community through their corporate citizenship. (Lumpkin *et al.*, 2010; Le Breton-Miller, Miller, and Bares, 2015). However, what is still to be revealed is how the nature of the customer base and specific socio-political context influences corporate citizenship strategies of firms. This aspect is addressed later in our case study as well.

Role of the Family Values

Next to shareholder pressure, prior literature has also highlighted that (family) value orientation in family firms tends to positively influence corporate citizenship-oriented behaviour (e.g. Hammann *et al.*, 2009; Le Breton-Miller and Miller, 2016). Likewise, the ability of founders (owners) to enforce their personal values upon the family firms' strategic orientation (Koiranen, 2002; Aronoff and Ward, 2016) has been found as an important and contributory factor for corporate citizenship orientation (Le Breton-Miller and Miller, 2016). Relevant literature further suggests that family businesses exhibit values that reflect intergenerational aspirations. This makes them more embedded in their local communities (Koiranen, 2002; Aronoff and Ward, 2016), which further reinforces the importance and significance of these values. Family firms are inclined to undertake corporate citizenship initiatives due to a sense of responsibility towards local community as well as safeguarding intergenerational aspiration, as such initiatives ensure help and support from a range of stakeholders (e.g. Le Breton-Miller and Miller, 2016; Binz *et al.*, 2017). Hence, family values behind such firms' strategies play a significant role in the drive for corporate citizenship-oriented behaviour in such firms. It should further be noted that family values have a strong link to the aspects of the founder's background and experiences, as well as intergenerational aspirations, which are discussed in the next section.

Intergenerational Aspirations, Socioemotional Wealth and Founder's Role

Intergenerational aspirations, not just at level of values, but at the practical level also, are strongly linked to the overall reputation of a business as well as the family owners themselves, as reputation determines success or failure of business especially in this context (e.g. Koiranen, 2002;

74 *Arslan et al.*

Deephouse and Jaskiewicz, 2013). Block and Wagner (2014: 477) note that "family firms emphasize harmony and strive to maintain the heritage of their founders." This is a relatively important feature of corporate citizenship behaviour that has broad-level influence. The first level of influence is from the business founder themselves, as the value that they place on corporate citizenship underpins the firm's corporate citizenship strategy. For example, Binz *et al.*, (2017) describe how families with 'other-oriented' attitudes, or stewardship culture were inclined to facilitate the welfare of others and recognize the wide-ranging benefits of a corporate citizenship orientation. They continue that such prioritizing of non-financial goals reflects family culture generally introduced by the founder (Binz *et al.*, 2017, see also Cabeza-García *et al.*, 2017).

Second, the tendency to uphold legacy and ensure continuation drives family firms towards long-term orientation. This long-term orientation connects the reputation and reputational advantage that is recognized as key "resources" for family firms (e.g. Habbershon and Williams, 1999; Zellweger and Nason, 2008; Le Breton-Miller, Miller, and Bares, 2015). This is important since an important outcome of a positive reputation through corporate citizenship is socioemotional wealth. Socioemotional wealth includes having the family name associated with the emotional attachment to the firm, and the pride and satisfaction of family members working for the organisation (Gomez-Mejia *et al.*, 2011). It is primarily a non-financial benefit that satisfies a family's need associated with the influence and affinity in the local context resulting from corporate citizenship initiatives (Berrone *et al.*, 2012). Hence, socioemotional wealth resulting from corporate citizenship supports intergenerational aspirations and offers intangible long-term benefits to family firms.

However, as also indicated above to some extent, the findings of individual studies are still somewhat inconclusive, specifically regarding the financial outcomes of reputation advantages. Prior research has offered varying results in this area due to variance in context and circumstances of family firms in which the research has been conducted (Gomez-Mejia *et al.*, 2011). Likewise, the role of the founders also seems to be relevant, but still somewhat limitedly understood (e.g. Block and Wagner, 2014; Cabeza-García *et al.*, 2017). Therefore, we believe that there is value in examining these issues further in empirical settings. We also believe that qualitative case studies can provide much-needed insight that complements the general patterns found in more quantitatively oriented studies in the specific context of family firms (e.g. Fletcher *et al.*, 2016).

In the following case study, we analyse interplay between all these factors in the case of a family firm which operates in medical supplies service sector.

Introduction to the Case Firm: Medkit

The primary data from our case firm was collected using open-ended detailed interviews with the firm's founder and strategic manager. The interview followed all the themes covered in the theoretical overview and was transcribed in verbatim and analysed. Moreover, supplementary material from the case firm's website was used as receive additional information for the analysis and discussion. The founder and CEO, Ms. Minna Åman-Toivio, established MedKit in 2008. Her husband, a co-founder, MD Tuukka Toivio, has been working in many countries, in various circumstances, helping the victims in war and disaster areas, such as the Afghanistan war and Thailand tsunami. While operating abroad, they realized that some of the first aid products were either not available in Finland or were more expensive compared to prices in other countries. Following this observation, the firm started to import suitable, high-quality products from manufacturers, and had some of the products tailor-made under the MedKit label. MedKit orders the products from abroad and imports them to its warehouse located in Oulu, Finland, and then collects, packages, and ships the items to its customers. Effortless ordering, investments in customer experience, and fast deliveries have brought MedKit notable growth potential. The steady growth, both in terms of the number of customers and sales per customer, in turn, has permitted the firm to shift from relatively small deliveries to more extensive supply contracts. In 2019, the firm's turnover is approximately EUR 4 million and MedKit employed 15 staff, all of them working in Oulu, Finland (MedKit, 2019). At present, MedKit supplies over 6000 first aid, first care, and medical safety product items. MedKit has over 3800 healthcare, industrial, and private customers, mainly in Finland, although the firm delivers products also internationally to countries including civil war-ravaged countries, like Somalia.

Corporate Citizenship in Medkit

Corporate citizenship initiatives in the case firm are mostly self-initiated, as the founder strongly believes in paying back to the society with which she feels closely associated. The founder revealed that even though the medical supplies sector is highly competitive, corporate citizenship initiatives are helpful to gain prominence in the eyes of stakeholders. In the case of MedKit, corporate citizenship initiatives primarily revolve around offering students work practice positions and theses writing opportunities (e.g. bachelor's and master's theses at the end of undergraduate university studies), as well as offering work placements to long term unemployed people (including both senior and younger citizens). They train these unemployed individuals, upskilling them in areas such as digital marketing, data analytics, and Microsoft Power BI (business intelligence) visualisations

76 Arslan et al.

among others, thereby increasing their job prospects in other companies after going through training and work experience with MedKit.

The owner is very passionate about work experience opportunities and the relative lack of opportunities for young people, as most firms tend to look for experienced professionals. In many other western developed economies, including Finland, job opportunities and work placements for young people – particularly millennials – confront globalisation, outsourcing, and technological advancements (Bynner, Chisholm, and Furlong, 2018). The founder of the case firm feels rather personal and passionate about this topic as her own children are in this age cohort, and she feels that her generation should be willing to support the workforce of the future. This is a very important aspect as it touches upon the issue of the generational rift that has been the focus of recent discussions by many social researchers. Young people in developed western economies feel squeezed out of opportunities including jobs and housing by baby boomer generation (Weil *et al.*, 2017; Pickard, 2019). Hence, it was very clear that in case of firm, the founder's vision and family values played a significant role in developing corporate citizenship initiatives surrounding skills development and job market opportunities for young people, as well as other unemployed individuals and groups. Millennials are visible in the top management team of MedKit as well, thereby offering them leadership traits development opportunities. In the case of MedKit, corporate citizenship is part of corporate philosophy and organisational routine.

As a result, MedKit has received significant applause from relevant stakeholders including the President of Finland, the city of Oulu, and Business Oulu. These kinds of corporate strategies also strengthen the argument presented recently by researchers on the future of the welfare state and the voluntary involvement of the private sector. This kind of activity is relevant in making it easier for Nordic countries to preserve their current standards of living (Larsson *et al.*, 2012). In particular, while socioemotional wealth has been linked with family firm's need for affinity in the local context (e.g. Berrone *et al.*, 2012), linking socioemotional wealth to the larger picture of the socio-political context of a country (Nordic welfare state in the current case) is an important finding. In fact, the MedKit founder specifically highlighted this aspect and said that she has lived in the USA and the Middle East, and based on her experiences, she strongly supports and values of the Nordic welfare state model. She also referred to the long-term benefits for firms once they get involved in such ingenuities. For example, MedKit's educational program for the long-term unemployed people offers them work placements and job market skills that have benefited other stakeholders by sharing best practices, which further enhances the positive reputation of MedKit. The benefits may not always accrue directly but may realize through more indirect paths.

The case analysis also supported the argument presented in prior studies that family firms are more embedded in local society, and view the betterment of local society as a cornerstone for their own long-term success (e.g. Berrone *et al.*, 2012; Crane and Matten, 2016). The MedKit founder agreed with this concern. She highlighted that businesses need to take into account the social context where they operate. Along with corporate citizenship initiatives discussed so far, the founder referred to taxation honesty as very important. She referred to cases of large multinational firms, who have been highlighted in this context both globally and more locally in Finland. Taxation brings welfare, which is an important point and can be linked to some prior research done on taxation dynamics and differences between family and non-family firms (e.g. Mares, 2006; Flora, 2017). This finding can also be linked with earlier discussion on socioemotional wealth, as honesty in taxation can also potentially add to it; as an aspect, not addressed specifically in most prior studies on this topic.

The discussion also highlighted that although direct financial benefits of corporate citizenship are rather negligible, the founder is very happy and satisfied with reputational advantages and the socioemotional wealth that they generate. In her view, and in line with other above observations, these reputational advantages indirectly influence future business opportunities while dealing with both public sector hospitals, as well as private sector hospitals. It was revealed that due to reputational advantages, MedKit has received additional consulting projects outside the main areas of business from private sector healthcare organisations, as they viewed it as a trustworthy partner. Moreover, intergenerational aspirations were also visible in the case of MedKit, as the owner would like her children to continue to run the business. She feels that reputational advantages and socioemotional wealth, will help them in carrying on this useful legacy. Hence, our case offered support to prior studies, which also highlighted long term benefits of reputational advantages.

As a final point, like mentioned also earlier, specificities of the Nordic or Scandinavian context was visible in our case study. However, also another interesting aspect related to it emerged regarding role of family firms in the discussion. The founder was proud of welfare state of Finland and stressed the need to keep it going and highlighted the role that businesses (particularly family firms) need to play for this purpose. This finding is in line with some prior studies that have emphasized the importance of social responsibility and corporate citizenship for Nordic family-owned firms and done this with specific reference to the sociocultural and historical factors associated with the development of the relevant market economy and governance model (e.g. Iversen and Thue, 2008). We believe that this is an important finding that should be further analysed in limitedly explored contexts of emerging economies to see if similar trends and associations can be observed or not. Based on the discussion associated

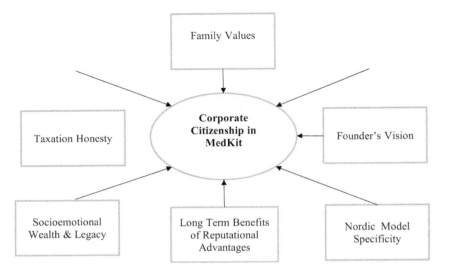

Figure 4.1 Overview of Corporate Citizenship Drivers in MedKit.

with our case firm, the following Figure 4.1 presents key characteristics of corporate citizenship in this specific context.

Implications, Limitations and Future Research Directions

The purpose of this study was to address and analyse corporate citizenship, and especially observe this phenomenon in a specific context of a Finnish family-owned firm operating in the medical supplies sector. We linked the findings to the wider debate on corporate citizenship by (family) firms and its role in a specific socio-political context. Based on our single case study, we can identify several useful implications for theory and the managerial audience.

A key theoretical implication relates to incorporating the model of governance and socio-political context into the debate on corporate citizenship in family, as well as potentially non-family owned, firms. A significant share of prior research on family firms and corporate citizenship has been conducted in the American context, with unique institutional and cultural characteristics (e.g. Block and Wagner, 2014). Our study findings are in line with prior studies done in the Nordic context, where the specificities of the Nordic (Scandinavian) model emerge in the discussion about corporate citizenship – especially the continuation of the welfare state model. Incorporation of socio-political context and governance model is expected to strengthen theoretical bases of extant corporate citizenship literature. Another theoretical implication relates to increased emphasis on the role of firms in skill development and employment dynamics in an economy. This is in line with larger debate on increased role of private sector in areas like these which were earlier viewed solely from public sector lens.

We also incorporate some current societal trends in our discussion on corporate citizenship. For example, in the case firm, the issue of generational rift in developed western economies (specifically fewer employment opportunities for young people), was one of the factors behind specific corporate citizenship initiatives. This calls for scholars to look beyond traditional issues like donations, charity, etc. (see, e.g. Block and Wagner, 2014) and expand to other issues, that may be more "mundane", everyday-issues that are hiding in plain sight. Examining the founder's vision, family values, and intergenerational aspirations is needed, especially when addressing corporate citizenship dynamics in family firms. Moreover, these aspects are influenced specifically by the founder's experiences, as exposure to societies with different levels of economic development, equality, and welfare regimes can influence perceptions towards corporate citizenship. This was also visible in our case firm.

Finally, reputational advantages emanating from corporate citizenship should be seen in overall perspective of business growth and new opportunities rather than merely focusing on short term monetary gains. We found that a firm that gains a positive reputation may also indirectly benefit by receiving business opportunities in business areas beyond their core interests. For example, while public and private actors may have initially different expectations for family firms, they may become tightly intertwined when a long-term approach is adopted.

Our study also offers some practical insights. In particular, family firms do not need to take an extravagant approach to corporate citizenship in order to gain benefits. As in the case of MedKit, merely living up to the established rules (e.g. paying taxes as is expected) and taking a strategic view on issues that companies need to do anyway (e.g. offering training and development opportunities, but paying attention to the immediate needs of the firm) can offer a family firm competitive advantage. It is up to the founders and family members in the organisation to make their values visible in their statements, and in their actions. Another point, that embracing the broad variety in their customer base, may provide family firms with opportunities to promote their business. Public and private sector customers (organisations) may have very different views on the family firm and may require it to take upon quite different actions; however, in the end, the reputational advantages and socioemotional wealth result in useful outcomes in both customer segments for family firms. The study also revealed that embeddedness in society may not bring short-term benefits, yet, the increased competitiveness emerges in the long run. Employment of young people, students, and long-term unemployed people require continuous commitment, but also builds reputational

80   *Arslan et al.*

advantage as well as pool of skilled workforce. Furthermore, long term profitable growth of any firm can be easily ruined by breaking the laws, for example by avoiding taxes. This aspect needs the specific attention of managers as increasingly external stakeholders including governments and media are becoming strict on this issue.

Finally, we need to acknowledge that like other academic endeavours, our study has limitations as well. First, it is a single case study on a family firm operating in a specific industrial sector, which makes generalisation of the findings problematic. However, we chose this firm due to it being engaged in best practices associated with corporate citizenship and receiving recognition and applause for it. We believe that future studies can build upon our work by specifically focusing on socio-political external factors like the governance model of countries and role of corporate sector in this context as highlighted in our findings. These future studies can analyse these in context of family firms operating in other industries and countries. Both qualitative and quantitative methodologies can be used in this work. Moreover, analysis of inter-relationship between the type of governance model in a country and corporate citizenship requires further investigation by scholars, as it would help to categorize macro level antecedents and influences properly for different types of economies. As corporate citizenship in family firms is an emerging concept, we have developed a table which highlights further areas of research and questions, which future studies can address specifically, along with the above-mentioned topics. Table 4.1 provides some suggestions on how to advance knowledge on these issues.

Table 4.1 Possible Topics for Future Studies

Research Question/Topic	Context	Methodology
How corporate citizenship dynamics vary in firms located in economic hubs (main cities) compared to firms located in peripheral regions?	Developed economies of western Europe and North America	Qualitative research methods
Analysis of the link between corporate citizenship and cultural dimensions of the society (country). It would be especially interesting to focus on the cultural dimensions from GLOBE cultural project like performance orientation, humane orientation and future orientation.	Both developed and emerging economies.	Both quantitative and qualitative research methods

(Continued)

Table 4.1 (Continued)

Research Question/Topic	Context	Methodology
The role of corporate citizenship in family firms to achieve the United Nations' (UN) sustainable development goals (SDGs) as most firms in the world are family-owned.	Both developed and emerging economies.	Both quantitative and qualitative methods.Multilevel analysis
Reputational benefits and their influence on business performance in the long run vs. short run: Comparison of corporate citizenship in family firms in different industries and service sectors.	Both developed and emerging economies	Both quantitative and qualitative methods.
Analysis of policy perspectives the corporate citizenship in family firms. Is this specific topic being recognised as important due to its usefulness in addressing certain pertaining social issues or is it still marginal issue in that specific context?	Developed economies	Exploratory qualitative studies.

References

Aronoff, C. and Ward, J. (2016) *Family business governance: Maximizing family and business potential.* New York: Springer.

Arregle, J.L. *et al.* (2007) 'The development of organizational social capital: Attributes of family firms', *Journal of Management Studies*, 44(1), pp. 73–95.

Baschieri, G., Carosi, A. and Mengoli, S. (2017) 'Family firm local involvement and the Local Home Bias phenomenon', *Long Range Planning*, 50(1), pp. 93–107.

Berrone, P., Cruz, C. and Gomez-Mejia, L.R. (2012) 'Socioemotional wealth in family firms: Theoretical dimensions, assessment approaches, and agenda for future research', *Family Business Review*, 25(3), pp. 258–279.

Binz, C.A. *et al.* (2017) 'Family business goals, corporate citizenship behaviour and firm performance: Disentangling the connections', *International Journal of Management and Enterprise Development*, 16(1–2), pp. 34–56.

Block, J.H. and Wagner, M. (2014) 'The effect of family ownership on different dimensions of corporate social responsibility: Evidence from large US firms', *Business Strategy and the Environment*, 23(7), pp. 475–492.

Bynner, J., Chisholm, L. and Furlong, A. (eds.). (2018) *Youth, citizenship and social change in a European context.* London: Routledge.

Cabeza-García, L., Sacristán-Navarro, M. and Gómez-Ansón, S. (2017) 'Family involvement and corporate social responsibility disclosure', *Journal of Family Business Strategy*, 8(2), pp. 109–122.

82 *Arslan et al.*

Campopiano, G. and De Massis, A. (2015) 'Corporate social responsibility reporting: A content analysis in family and non-family firms', *Journal of Business Ethics*, 129(3), pp. 511–534.

Carney, M. *et al.* (2015) 'What do we know about Private Family Firms? A meta–analytical review', *Entrepreneurship Theory and Practice*, 39(3), pp. 513–544.

Crane, A. and Matten, D. (2016) *Business ethics: Managing corporate citizenship and sustainability in the age of globalization.* Oxford: Oxford University Press.

Cruz, C. *et al.* (2014) 'Are family firms really more socially responsible?', *Entrepreneurship Theory and Practice*, 38(6), pp. 1295–1316.

Deephouse, D.L. and Jaskiewicz, P. (2013) 'Do family firms have better reputations than non-family firms? An integration of socioemotional wealth and social identity theories', *Journal of Management Studies*, 50(3), pp. 337–360.

De Massis, A. *et al.* (2015) 'Product innovation in family versus nonfamily firms: An exploratory analysis', *Journal of Small Business Management*, 53(1), pp. 1–36.

Famiyeh, S. (2017) 'Corporate social responsibility and firm's performance: empirical evidence', *Social Responsibility Journal*, 13(2), pp. 390–406.

Fletcher, D., De Massis, A. and Nordqvist, M. (2016) 'Qualitative research practices and family business scholarship: A review and future research agenda', *Journal of Family Business Strategy*, 7(1), pp. 8–25.

Flora, P. (2017) *Development of welfare states in Europe and America.* Oxon: Routledge.

Gardberg, N.A. and Fombrun, C.J. (2006) 'Corporate citizenship: Creating intangible assets across institutional environments', *Academy of Management Review*, 31(2), pp. 329–346.

Glavas, A. and Piderit, S.K. (2009) 'How does doing good matter? Effects of corporate citizenship on employees', *Journal of Corporate Citizenship*, 36, pp. 51–70.

Gomez-Mejia, L.R. *et al.* (2011) 'The bind that ties: Socioemotional wealth preservation in family firms', *Academy of Management Annals*, 5(1), pp. 653–707.

Gudmundson, D., Hartman, E.A. and Tower, C.B. (1999) 'Strategic orientation: Differences between family and nonfamily firms', *Family Business Review*, 12(1), pp. 27–39.

Galbreath, J. (2006) 'Corporate social responsibility strategy: Strategic options, global considerations', *Corporate Governance: The International Journal of Business in Society*, 6(2), pp. 175–187.

Gallo, M.Á., Tàpies, J. and Cappuyns, K. (2004) 'Comparison of family and nonfamily business: Financial logic and personal preferences', *Family Business Review*, 17(4), pp. 303–318.

Gavana, G., Gottardo, P. and Moisello, A. (2017) 'Earnings management and CSR disclosure. Family vs. non-family firms', *Sustainability*, 9(12), pp. 2327.

Habbershon, T.G. and Williams, M.L. (1999) 'A resource-based framework for assessing the strategic advantages of family firms', *Family Business Review*, 12(1), pp. 1–25.

Hammann, E.M., Habisch, A. and Pechlaner, H. (2009) 'Values that create value: socially responsible business practices in SMEs–empirical evidence from German companies', *Business Ethics: A European Review*, 18(1), pp. 37–51.

Hammond, N.L., Pearson, A.W. and Holt, D.T. (2016) 'The quagmire of legacy in family firms: Definition and implications of family and family firm legacy orientations', *Entrepreneurship Theory and Practice*, 40(6), pp. 1209–1231.

Halme, M. and Laurila, J. (2009) 'Philanthropy, integration or innovation? Exploring the financial and societal outcomes of different types of corporate responsibility', *Journal of Business Ethics*, 84(3), pp. 325–339.

Iversen, M.J. and Thue, L. (2008) *Creating Nordic capitalism–The business history of a competitive periphery*. Basingstoke: Palgrave Macmillan, pp. 1–19.

Jaskiewicz, P., Combs, J.G. and Rau, S.B. (2015) 'Entrepreneurial legacy: Toward a theory of how some family firms nurture transgenerational entrepreneurship', *Journal of Business Venturing*, 30(1), pp. 29–49.

Kelly, L.M., Athanassiou, N. and Crittenden, W.F. (2000) 'Founder centrality and strategic behavior in the family-owned firm', *Entrepreneurship Theory and Practice*, 25(2), pp. 27–42.

Koiranen, M. (2002) 'Over 100 years of age but still entrepreneurially active in business: Exploring the values and family characteristics of old Finnish family firms', *Family Business Review*, 15(3), pp. 175–187.

Larsson, B., Letell, M. and Thörn, H. (2012) 'Transformations of the Swedish welfare state: Social engineering, governance and governmentality', in *Transformations of the Swedish welfare state*. London: Palgrave Macmillan, pp. 3–22.

Le Breton-Miller, I., Miller, D. and Bares, F. (2015) 'Governance and entrepreneurship in family firms: Agency, behavioral agency and resource-based comparisons', *Journal of Family Business Strategy*, 6(1), pp. 58–62.

Le Breton-Miller, I. and Miller, D. (2016) 'Family firms and practices of sustainability: A contingency view', *Journal of Family Business Strategy*, 7(1), pp. 26–33.

Lumpkin, G.T., Brigham, K.H. and Moss, T.W. (2010) 'Long-term orientation: Implications for the entrepreneurial orientation and performance of family businesses', *Entrepreneurship & Regional Development*, 22(3-4), pp. 241–264.

Maignan, I. and Ferrell, O.C. (2000) 'Measuring corporate citizenship in two countries: The case of the United States and France. *Journal of Business Ethics*, 23(3), pp. 283–297.

Matten, D., Crane, A. and Chapple, W. (2003) 'Behind the mask: Revealing the true face of corporate citizenship', *Journal of Business Ethics*, 45(1–2), pp. 109–120.

Mares, I. (2006) *Taxation, wage bargaining, and unemployment*. Cambridge: Cambridge University Press.

MedKit (2019) https://blog.medkit.fi/fi/medkitilla-onnistunut-kasvun-vuosi-yritys-jatkoi-vahvaa-kasvuaan.

Miller, D. *et al.* (2018) 'Strategic distinctiveness in family firms: Firm institutional heterogeneity and configurational multidimensionality', *Journal of Family Business Strategy*, 9(1), pp. 16–26.

Neubauer, F. and Lank, A.G. (2016) *The family business: Its governance for sustainability*. UK: Palgrave Macmillan.

Pickard, S. (2019) 'Age war as the new class war? Contemporary representations of intergenerational inequity', *Journal of Social Policy*, 48(2), pp. 369–386.

Saeed, M.M. and Arshad, F. (2012) 'Corporate social responsibility as a source of competitive advantage: The mediating role of social capital and reputational capital', *Journal of Database Marketing & Customer Strategy Management*, 19(4), pp. 219–232.

Waddock, S. and Smith, N. (2000) 'Relationships: The real challenge of corporate global citizenship', *Business and Society Review*, 105(1), pp. 47–62.

Weil, S.W., Wildemeersch, D. and Percy-Smith, B. (2017) *Unemployed youth and social exclusion in Europe: Learning for inclusion?* Oxon: Routledge.

Zahra, S.A., Hayton, J.C. and Salvato, C. (2004) 'Entrepreneurship in family vs. non-family firms: a resource–based analysis of the effect of organizational culture', *Entrepreneurship Theory and Practice*, 28(4), pp. 363–381.

Zellweger, T.M. and Nason, R.S. (2008) 'A stakeholder perspective on family firm performance', *Family Business Review*, 21(3), pp. 203–216.

5 Family Businesses, Family Values and Corporate Citizenship

Paroma Sen and Ipshita Adhikary

In this chapter, we focus on family values in shaping family businesses and in the context also try to see the rise of corporate citizenship getting affected by the same values. Pre-colonial rule and colonialism could rule over the Indian subcontinent because of the division of the society into smaller communities. It was the survival of individuals within groups based on family values that overpowered all other values. Family became the central force in shaping choices and also making decisions. Businesses were also an outcome rather than the extension of the same belief system. The classes based on the caste system also divided groups; among these groups that were dominant were the businesses communities such as the Gujaratis, Sindhis and Marwaris. These groups also had a strong policy of endogamous business extending in their business interactions only within groups. It was not the forces of the market that shaped the outcome of a business but the community that played a central role and, as a result, in face of failure of the market the damage was not borne by a single firm or individual but it became a failure for the group/community, as a whole, resulting in extended support being granted to the owner of a single business. In this context, the role of the state protecting its citizen through welfare was substituted by community support instead. Group-based support provided to the individual members of the group led to the absence of any contemplation with regard to role of business in extending welfare to corporate citizens. However, to completely overlook the role of the business class in supporting corporate citizens would be tantamount to not recognising their role as business communities in social reforms during the colonial rule. Business communities supported social reforms by opening schools, hospitals etc., and on some other occasions, they also played an important role in addressing issues of women with their emphasis on schooling, especially for girls.

Businesses in India started with philanthropic work during the nationalist movement in order to counter the foreign capitalist control under the colonial rule. Communities such as Marwaris, Gujratis and others offered support to the nationalist leaders to resist the continuance

DOI: 10.4324/9780429281228-6

86   *Paroma Sen and Ipshita Adhikary*

of foreign rule. Resisting the foreign domination was made possible by the nationalist leaders with the help of the business communities; involved in addressing the social backwardness of the country. A reform at the social level was in the form of schooling, widow remarriage or any other reform addressing the issue of inequalities. Communities were largely driven by their family values and extending social welfare to support the nationalist cause was also done by remaining within the value-based framework of the families. Extending any form of support meant a continuation of traditions agreed amongst the members of the same family. All these group-based values could not shape the ideas of citizenship based on political, social and economic rights. As a result, the social rights of a citizen for a long were not an outcome of the corporate citizenship of the businesses. Instead, the shift in the trend happened with the passing of the corporate social responsibility, made mandatory with the amendment in The Company Act, 2013.

We intend to explore the changes in the family values over the period through a theoretical, as well as, an empirical perspective. This paper will be focusing on the changes in Indian business families post-globalization alongside the impact of corporate social responsibility in changing the perception of family-owned businesses towards corporate citizenship.

State, Society, and Economy

In this section, we look into the interconnection between state, society and economy in India. Any change in the structure of economy could not remove the influence of social structures upon it. Since the hierarchies of the society determined the economic outcomes unlike vice-versa, the communities and their practices within society became a force to reckon with. India's diversity became its strength but also a reason for not a linear development for any change. The formal spaces were influenced largely by informal interactions. The ideas of citizenship along with its additional duties were not placing the citizen in direct interface with the state. As a result, the citizen was simultaneously a member of the society and state. While this phenomenon could be common in other places, in India especially in case of economic development the ideas of homo-economicus had to be redefined. The rational optimizing side of the human being was not independent of social influences and categories. Such a phenomenon in India dates back to the rise of commercial law in Medieval India. With the rise of the modern nation-state, the rise of laws became immanent to provide a framework and rules to guide the governance of the society. From that perspective, the framework had to be codified, written and was thought would eventually transform the lives of the human beings. But interestingly, there could be a case-specific to this part of the world where laws have survived even without being codified and rather being communicated through everyday practices and followed by others without any precedence. In all of these developments what influenced this phenomenon was social trust that held communities together. However, one also needs to take into account that faith existed only among members of the community along with the lack of trust towards non-members. Here, linking this idea with social life and loyalty becomes important, according to Russell, 'Social life is mechanical, precise and static' and it was precise because of this that individuals wanted to remain a part of social life amongst known people than amongst the unknown and along with this loyalty also remained equally significant. Group loyalty also links the place of the individual within a society with that of state. Initially, group-based loyalties gave rise to solidarity that was free of fear, which was replaced by obedience out of fear. It was in the latter case that there was this rise of state-building. From here on we make two significant distinctions between economic development within society and that within the state. The following arguments show that decision making may not be always an outcome of rationality. Rationality could also be linked to solidarity and economic activity to that of social trust. Now, in explaining trust one needs to understand it in the context of Medieval India.

In Medieval India, trust was an outcome of social behaviour. This social behaviour was an outcome of *Dharma*. Unlike the Constitution of the modern state, it was *Dharma* that placed limits on the behaviour of individuals including rulers. In the process of imposition of limits, certain texts have sanctioned economic division of caste from this perspective. *Dharmashastras* have gone ahead to link economic activities with the caste system in India. Practising commerce and trade was the work of the Vaishyas. These distinctions led to allowing certain practices by Vaishyas but not by Brahmins such as banking. These developments led to the creation of a personalized economic sphere unlike commonly accepted system of a depersonalized economic sphere (Davis and Donald, 2005). In a way, the framework followed in an economy was that of personalized mutual trust and expectation (Davis and Donald, 2005). Dharma may not have a western synonym and hence; one may not also consider it to be a virtue of the western world. Laws without texts and their multiple interpretations at various levels – family, community and society – led to emphasis being laid on '*maintaining order*'. This order was termed *Dharma* and was followed in various enclaves with different interpretations. In addition to this, there were several prescribed orders by the sages in the form of *Dharmashastras*. Robert Lingat in his seminal work states, "*Dharma rests primarily and essentially upon the Veda or rather upon Revelations (sruti). The Vedic texts are really revealed texts, divine words gathered directly by the inspired bards, the risis. They consists of three collections of liturgical texts particularly named 'Vedas': the Rig Veda, the Sama-veda and the Yajur-veda, to which a fourth collection,*

88 *Paroma Sen and Ipshita Adhikary*

the Atharva-veda, was added at some later date". In Hinduism, the concept of *Dharma* differed from one another. The Laws of Manu which influenced Hindu society survived through tensions between continuity and discontinuity. Hindu society was an aggregation of epistemic realities of human beings, order and chaos; pattern and disjunctures. As a result, the business also became specific economic activity for certain communities over others. There are religious and caste overlaps in defining these business traits within communities but for a precise take on this paper, we start with the rise of Dharmashastras and its influence on the business environment in the medieval era. It is crucial at this stage to understand to what extent similar practices were present in the western world. Dharma enters into the economic discussion in the west in the name of virtue. Bringing in the western concept of ethics, one focuses on virtues, as explained, by various thinkers. On the one hand, Aristotle focused on harmony and on the other hand, Nietzche focused on assertiveness as an example of virtue in business. Then it also brings forth the issue of efficiency of the market and how this also contributes to morality. Morality could only be achieved if there is harmony with the rest of the society (Frederick, 1999). Corporate citizenship could then be seen as giving rise to two different perspectives: one is that of harmony as propounded by the rule of Dharma and another through morality focusing on the harmony in balancing an egoistic self with the collective needs of the other. According to the medieval interpretation, the stability then was a result of harmony within groups in a society and in case of western morality, the stability emerges from the cooperation between self and the other. So there is a very different kind of balancing that is at play. However, with the rise of globalization and the emergence of an interdependent economy, one realizes that society has undergone a massive change in the economic sphere which has further led to new forms of conflict and cooperation. Now bringing the debate back to the economic space in the country and the group-centric loyalties, one notices that along with caste there were community-centric loyalties that allowed the rise of businesses and their success in India.

Business Communities: Interface between Traditions and Customs

The economy of a place is shaped by the practices in a particular religion. Weber, rightly put this argument into perspective when he compared the rise of capitalism with puritanism in Christianity. The regularity of doing something over and over again, as in religion, affect the economic life of the middle-class population. Both religion and economy of capitalism followed by the middle class emphasised savings over wastage. Unlike the feudal class and aristocracy, the middle class believed in savings and investment through which they wanted to counter destitution. In

Family Values and Corporate Citizenship 89

Protestant Ethics, Weber quotes that 'We all know the type of modern businessman who likes to make use of the old saying *"the people must have religion"*... branding these businessmen as *"clerical police"* when it comes to branding strikes as sinful and accusing the trades unions of encouraging *"covetousness"*...' (Weber, p. 50). This is quite similar to the *Dharma*, being the guiding force in India among business communities, which also took the role of providing guidelines to be followed for doing business. Similar to the business philosophy that prevailed among the communities in India of securing the results of benefit not just in the temporal world but beyond, in *Protestant Ethics* one finds that middle-class life was influenced by phrases such as *"to make the best of both worlds"* and following the *"idea of calling"*. And through this connection between religion and economy, focus shifts from class-based inequalities. As inequality could not be an outcome of the capitalistic mode of production as creation of wealth was not an aim of capitalistic production seen from a religious vantage point. Wealthy men instead of amassing wealth should use it for a better purpose. This was further emphasised by religious precepts valuing 'ceaseless, constant, systematic labour' (ibid., p. 116). The Puritan philosophy of life as noted by Weber benefitted the middle class; with their emphasis on containing temptations for wealth and instead focus on economically rational conduct of life. (ibid., p. 117). This spirit of capitalism could be compared to the philosophy of life as followed among the business communities in India. In both these cases, it was not the mathematical formula that helped them take risks but rather a philosophy of social and religious life. Business communities and castes in India oriented their successors towards a tradition of trade by focusing on their psychological make-up through 'n-affiliation' which was determined by networking with their fellow caste members (Timberg, p. 72). The spirit of capitalism as embraced in the West was to follow their class order which was replaced by caste order in India. In both the cases, achievements in business meant following an order, creating networks and upholding a spirit to carry out the function of business. For instance, in India while Marwaris, business communities with roots in Rajasthan, formed networks with their community brethren other communities such as Mahisya caste dealing with small engineering shops among Bengalis from Howrah district of present West Bengal networked with their caste fellows (ibid). While business communities continued to do business and form networks within their endogamous groups, risk-taking was given equal importance. Family networks led to instilling faith and encouraging collaboration. Networking among the businesses communities in India meant greater faith among the known collaborators and the decision on these lines were taken by the family as a whole with no separation of power between management and ownership. The success of the business was not based on whether the products could be better marketed by the

90   *Paroma Sen and Ipshita Adhikary*

managers of the company. And in these lines, Aditya Birla said, "I have nothing against MBAs. They are brilliant boys, extremely bright and enterprising. There is nothing wrong with the man, but the training given is better suited for multinationals..." This brings to the fore a clear distinction between family-led businesses and multinational companies (ibid., p. 77). And as a result, while philanthropy was a part of business ethics more closely tied to religious and traditional values of business families in the colonial times especially during the nationalist struggle of the country, the role of management-driven corporate social responsibility was a phenomenon of the post globalized world. For instance, the Triple Bottom Line Reporting (also known as TBL) became a framework in the management terms for measuring an organization's performance along with the social, economic and environmental yardsticks. On the lines of Weberian thought that economic situations are a result of traditions of a particular place, the organizational theorists may not focus on traditions, but they focus on the tendency of isomorphism. "Isomorphism means that the organizations takes in the same form as its environment" (Hatch and Cunliffe, 2006). For MNCs, in order to be successful, changing with the need of the environment was as important and reflecting on complex dependencies was also crucial. Moving beyond a familiar territory meant streamlining as per the regulations in place in a particular country. Population ecologists focus on organisation's ability to make the best selections out of given resources. To that end, organizations survive not through networking as happened in family-based businesses but through a combination of 'Variation, selection and retention'. Where variation meant responding to 'new threats and opportunities in their environments'; selection occurred when organizations thought their ability to survive was able to fit in the environment that supported it; finally adopting the ability to retention to constantly change by being more adaptable (ibid).

Traditions of Philanthropy across Business Communities

India lives within its communities; this was even true of business of this country. The economic history of business families shows how intrinsically the idea of business was closely linked to values held by families. While some business houses were prominent and became the face of the economic world, there were various small industries spread across the length and breadth of the country. Despite some shared values of doing business, there also were some embedded traits of communities distinguishing one from the other. For example, trade with areas outside India was common among Sindhis, Multanis and Parsis but not so common among Marwaris. Interestingly, the geographical location of these groups also influenced some of their business decisions. Multanis belonging to the region between Punjab and Sind in present-day Pakistan

Family Values and Corporate Citizenship 91

moved to Central Asian regions to spread their business. This approach was not common among the Marwaris community that moved towards the eastern part of the Indian subcontinent. Some other communities explored the possibilities of doing business in South East Asia. Such as the Harilela family belonging to the Sindhi community is into the third generation of doing business in Hong Kong. While they continue to uphold their Sindhi identity they have so well adapted themselves to their domiciled country that they consider themselves as Chinese Sindhis. Another way of upholding their Sindhi identity is by uplifting their communities back in India by contributing to philanthropic work. Philanthropy, as a social practice of giving back to the community, is a value they believe has been instilled within them by the elders of their families. Harilela brothers, one of the well-known industrialists of Indian origin belonging to the Sindhi community in Hong Kong. believed that success was giving back to society. Sending a part of what was earned for their community's development led to sending money back to India in the form of aid to education in Gujarat, distributing sewing machines and arranging mass weddings. Interestingly, within the Harilela family there were differences in opinion over the types of philanthropic activities to be undertaken. For instance, initiatives such as donating in "Kanya Daan Trust, which financed mass weddings for women in India who could not afford a dowry or the wedding expenses" was seen as supporting patriarchal practices by the current generation while it was seen as unburdening the family by the previous generation (Bathija, 2017). These values are not meant to uphold the modern concept of corporate social responsibility or doing something for a particular nation but have often been considered as community-centric sometimes even linked to their religious practices. Such practices of community-centric values towards philanthropy have a cosmopolitan approach that is in no way influenced by the role of the state. State and its laws in such cases have negligible influence as long as the work done is aimed at the welfare of the downtrodden. As a result, this approach to welfare was not restricted to corporate citizenship as per the laws of a state. It also shows that giving back to the community is not linked to the generation of any exchange value of any kind. So the management of the company is in no position or power to influence the decision-making of the owners of an organization regarding social contribution. Neither the profit-driven nor the brand-driven motives of the management could influence the satisfaction of the owners towards giving back to the community of their origin. However, the role of the state was not negligible as well since they also played a crucial role in shaping identities of the business communities. The Parsi community could spread their business in Europe because of the safeguard provided by the colonial state in commutation through the sea. Transportation of goods became possible through state protection given to business communities, minimizing the risk on the sea.

The Parsis collaborated with the company authorities who ensured 'safeguard of the coastal channels so as to keep them free from piracy (mostly on cotton boats) and to facilitate smooth business transactions up-country where conditions of war and strife occasionally impeded supplies' (Subramanian, 2016). Similarly, various protectionist measures were guaranteed by the colonial state in doing business with neighbouring countries. Export of cotton to China in exchange for tea became a business strategy for the British government. With the support of the colonial state Parsi community was also able to prosper in manufacturing of shipbuilding. At the same time, Parsis also converted their business wealth into that of charity (ibid). In some cases, the state-supported the growth of businesses and in other cases certain community-centric practices led to supporting the continuance of the state. "Already in the 14th century, Barani noted that Multanis were heavily invested in the textile trade while also serving as large-scale creditors for the Delhi Sultanate nobility" (Levi, 2016). In some places Multanis were merchants and in other places recognized as bankers. Banking system was linked to the success of a Marwari businessman named Jagat Seth. Among the Multanis, those who were engaged in business of money changers were referred to as Sarrafs. Banking system was based on a family-firm model which was also behind the success of their businesses as faith within them allowed wealth to be moved from one place to another (ibid).

Prospects of business are not just restricted to demand and supply of the market but also through the unhindered supply of capital. The growth of capital was not because of the banking system developed by the state. Business communities supported their kith and kin in business through a trust-based capital transfer. The presence of this banking system based on mutual trust led to a trust system that supported the continuance of businesses. Hundi system was almost like the modern-day bill of exchange, thereby, minimizing the risk involved in non-payment of loans with banks outside this community system. In other words, the mortgage-free banking system functioned because of the fear of losing trust in case of non-payment of loan amount within the pre-agreed stipulated time. While such a system of banking provided tremendous support base to the communities in the economic sphere, it also could not restrict the influence of the colonial state from laying the foundation of the banks such as the Punjab National Bank and Allahabad Bank.

Business history of a country emerges within a political context. Despite the opening of business opportunities for Indian business communities in India, there was a persistent struggle against the political control of country by the colonial powers. And as a result, the business groups had to extend their support towards the national cause of the country which could never be secondary to the economic interest.

Family Values and Corporate Citizenship   93

Political cause brought all the business groups together and Congress being the face of the national movement was supported by the major business groups in India. G.D Birla, Jamnalal Bajaj and others came out in support of the Congress to give a signal that they shared a common interest for the country. However, there were ideological divisions within Congress itself, which led to business groups being closer to leaders like Mahatma Gandhi and Vallabhbhai Patel over Jawaharlal Nehru. Closer to the independence of the country in 1947, the business groups came up with the Bombay Plan to articulate their policy initiative in the country and reaffirm the support of the state to their cause. Simultaneously, their role in addressing upliftment of the country through a commitment to social work led to reassuring the state of their support towards the cause of the country. However, leaders like Nehru with socialist bent of mind did not want to accept the business communities with open arms. As a result, in the post-independence era instead of acceptance, there was a prevalence of animosity between the state and the business groups. Private business groups were seen with suspicion and branded as groups primarily seeking profits over welfare of their people. More than the mere influence of the state, there was an interference of the state through introduction of licence-raj and thereby establishment of control over the business activities. At this stage, the state came to be seen as a welfare state, with the focus on social citizenship over corporate citizenship. The deliberate separation of the political welfare state from the business groups meant seeing the latter as the cause of much inequality in the country. It was a time when the Indian state in the process of following the Soviet-style industrialization led to emergence of the state-supported industrialization. All of these ended up giving rise to crony socialism and favouritism of certain groups over the other. Protectionism extended to firms enabled the state to create a safety net for the industrial groups from global competition. Pushing of industrial groups and the environment of suspicion drew a picture whereby, it was seen that business was meant only for profit. However, this led to a myopic view of the role of business in social transformation. While completely overlooking the fact that sustainability of business requires following ethics in business and winning the trust of the community within which the business groups are functioning. There was then an apparent compartmentalization between state, business and welfare. Welfare role had to betaken by the state for its citizens and this kind of a socialistic driven welfare politics looked at business from the point of view of exchange value only and overlooked the experiential value on which depended the sustainability of the market in the society. 'In ancient Greece, a person who refused to think in terms of the common good was called an *idiotis*-a privateer, a person who minded his own business' (Varoufakis, 2019). Taking on this point, one realizes even if market societies end up with a singular aim of earning profit, it may not ensure their long term sustainability- which is true of

94 *Paroma Sen and Ipshita Adhikary*

most democratic economies. It was not that the state could singularly impose welfare policies upon the members of a particular country without the consent of the rich business class but the rich business class too found welfare state to safeguard them. 'Even the rich began to realize that a welfare state was an excellent insurance policy against losing their property, their peace of mind, indeed their own heads. But the question then became: who pays for this? As we have previously noted, the rich never liked to pay the necessary taxes and the poor cannot afford to. So what then? (ibid., p. 151)'. Since profit-making was synonymous with business and welfare was associated with the state, both were seen as strange bedfellows. The role of the private companies was restricted to voluntary charity work but could not be conceived as partners in welfare programmes. While there exists the larger anti-business perception, there are also instances, such as Dilip Kumar Lakhi, involved in inter-generational trade-in diamonds who believes that 'Whenever a man thinks about tax evasion, he loses focus on his business' (Bathija, 2017). Mr. Dilip Kumar Lakhi, who happens to be one of the highest taxpayers in the country busted the myth that all successful businessmen are tax evaders. While there could be outliers, it was not because of the state guidelines that led the business houses to follow ethics which was rather considered necessary to stay in business. While the current business culture brought in formalism, Dilip Lakhi who followed the family rules ended up adopting an ethical path (ibid). It was not CSR (Corporate Social Responsibility) but the institutional values ingrained within families that created pressure of conforming to ethical practices. However, in the present form, Dilip Lakhi mentioned that his company is involved in an ABN AMRO project with the support of an NGO which work towards the rehabilitation of the street children (ibid).

Governance and Development

Corporate social responsibility was linked to the changing state policies towards business. During the colonial rule, the role of charity was restricted to the small groups of businesses classes who contributed towards the society under the influence of family customs. The interface between the state and business led to restricting a unified role of all businesses communities to contribute to the social cause effectively. Differences across business communities were exploited by the colonial state even when they tried to mediate between communities. For instance, Parsis and Hindus sought protection and support over issues of business with different rulers. While Paris wanted the intervention of the British the Hindus preferred the Marathas. Even when conflict remained unresolved, the British tried to bring in a unified system for their own convenience of doing trade with Indians (Roy, 2016). As a result, they brought in the coinage system and contract laws in India. Bringing in this uniformity was a way to move beyond traditional ways of doing business like the Hundi system followed among businesses communities. There was a shift from informal trust-based understanding to that of following the process of legal documentation. As a result, at different points in time since the time of colonial rule there were state made policies and legal rules to regulate the market economy. Another interesting aspect of economic development within country was the influence of external political-economic situation. For instance, the policy of protectionism led to gain for Indian capitalists during World War I. In the 1930s DCM (Delhi Cloth and General Mills Company) owners earned profit by selling tents and garments for the army during World War II. Another trend of the starting of Indo-European firms that had become common in India and has often been considered to be a post-globalization phase started long back in 1918, when two brothers named Gupta brought in the Britannia Biscuits in Calcutta. Similarly, there were others companies like the Martin Burns, which was an Indo-European firm founded in 1918, then Metal Box, or the starting the GKN (Guest, Keen and Williams) in Calcutta in 1920s. Along with the setting up of firms there was also the starting of corporate banking system in India, with the setting up of Punjab National Bank and Bank of Baroda. It was also a phase where the customary control of business in the hands of communities and families were overtaken by individuals; individuals without any background in business made a foray into business (Roy, 2016). Kwaja Abdul Hamied who taught at Allahabad University started the firm CIPLA (Chemical, Industrial and Pharmaceutical Laboratories Ltd) in 1935. Similarly, Laxmanrao Kirloskar, a teacher of mechanical drawings set up his engineering industries. All this contributes to the changing Indian landscape of business (ibid). As a result, the post-globalization phenomenon of investment by multinational companies, doing businesses with foreign firms are not something new for the country but has its precedent in the colonial past itself. However, the major change has been in the past everything was state-initiated which continues in the period of license raj in India to have undergone change in the present times. With globalization business itself focused on looking for certain standardized rules to be followed in India and abroad. Investments by foreign companies could be regulated by the state but not controlled. As a result, with FDI major changes also had to be brought in the process of doing charity by business groups. Charity by business communities was overtaken by standards; as a result, legal laws had to be established for businesses to undertake corporate social responsibility. This was also a long shift from the days of FERA (Foreign Exchange Management Act) era of 1973 to the 1980s. There was a move towards embracing the demands of the customers over following the customs. Following common standards led to not just focusing on the inequality in the society but also focusing on democratizing businesses.

96 *Paroma Sen and Ipshita Adhikary*

Moving beyond the socio-historical needs of a place the way the host country also allowed the entry of foreign firms. There was following a common standardized rule for all the countries of the world. In the process, the focus was on problems inflicting the entire world and not just a particular country. Issues of gender, poverty and environment have become the common issues taken up by corporate.

Post-globalization, economies of the world became interdependent. Along with this shift, capitalism in order to sustain itself soon realised the need to include social auditing to measure the company's growth. Somewhere growth and development could not work separately but the latter had to become a part of the former. Critics of capitalism might also rightly say that development of support or responsibility is taken up by the MNCs are also the ways to make inroads and gain support from the incumbent government that cannot be overlooked. Interestingly, there were transformations of the welfare state. Along with embracing the new era, adopting a new policy of governing led governments in democratic countries to give preference to governance. Somewhere, governance became an important factor for both political and economic sustenance. As a result, mutual acceptance of each other's presence by state and market led to changing the narrative of welfare in countries of the world. India after moving on the path of liberalization made scope for increased investment and business opportunities by the MNCs. While this resulted in an economic growth moving ahead of its earlier Hindu growth rate, it also went on to show an acceptance of the Washington Consensus. However, the aim of this paper is not to simplify the emergence of liberalization and reaffirming of capitalism, rather understand the changes in the dynamics of social responsibility undertaken by MNC's. While focusing on social responsibility the role played by the market was not intended to remove social inequality. But it was soon realised that it is essential to accept social equity to be an important part of growth. This led to a change in dynamics quite similar to other countries. With the rise in MNCs, increase in the size of organizations there was an overhaul within fiduciary organizations. Companies could not continue to limit their success based on profits earned and by upholding the interest of shareholders. The continuity in business meant maintaining a balance among all the stakeholders: consumers, shareholders, managers and owners. Increasingly, the business houses are not limited to decisions by the owners who earlier also were the managers. There is also an issue of agency, especially in cases where managers and owners are different. Along with the agency issue, emerges the internal politics between the board and managers leading to power politics over asymmetrical information. In the midst of all these, one can also see how philanthropy itself is undergoing a change. Philanthropy in its initial version was extended in support of the state, for instance, the support given to the nationalist struggle during the colonial period. It was not seen as making

Family Values and Corporate Citizenship 97

a way into areas where the active participation of the state started receding. On the contrary, at present, the state wants participation of the corporates in areas of development. There is certainly a two-pronged approach: one is addressing issues of development only from the perspectives of social gains and the other is to enable the foreign firms to perform to find acceptance within the country. With increased reliance on governance by the government, and it becomes a case for guaranteeing electoral victory for the government in power, the state prefers to share developmental outcomes with corporates. And with this huge shift in the functioning mechanism of the government, social responsibility or corporate citizenship is seen as a way to improve public delivery systems. Similarly, there has been a change in the functioning of the corporates where it is believed now that earning profits may not sustain a brand in the long run. In other words, the brand itself is created through social contribution. It is no more about optimizing the forces of production that are reducing the cost of production and guaranteeing benefit. Rather in order to attain benefit over cost, corporates are focusing on the need to increase the incidence of CSR. And in order to meet the demand for the right quality of public services, the state is resorting to partnerships with the private sectors. This approach has taken a new direction with shifts in organizations based on fiduciary relations amongst family groups. Indian firms started facing competition from companies outside India, as a result, philanthropy also became a strategy to remain relevant to the needs of the market. Governance also contributed to change in the welfare state policies with greater emphasis given to time-bound development strategies which could be supported with data. Evidence driven social responsibility replaced social rights. As a result, there was a decreasing dependence on affirming social rights of citizens and increasing emphasis on corporate citizenship. With the rise of corporate citizenship, the interface between the state and citizen underwent a change. Rights that were guaranteed by the state were a shield against any form of penury. With the rolling back of the state, onus if not being entirely shifted was traded off with the corporates.

Moral acceptance was projected as ethics in doing business. Ethics constituted a global standard of doing business accepted across the world. Indicators showing the ethics followed in business covered a wide range of issues from climate change, gender equality to the eradication of child labour etc. For instance, IKEA, which started its project in Uttar Pradesh, ensured a significant reduction in child labour in carpet manufacturing industries. In order to do so, IKEA also worked closely with other stakeholders in India. This phase of social responsibility focused on creating a network of governance in such a way that growth in economy could simultaneously guarantee development. And at the same time, development could be guaranteed not as a result of welfare programmes undertaken by family-based firms surviving on fiduciary ties, as in

Paroma Sen and Ipshita Adhikary

colonial times; but based on the strength of a global network addressing issues of rights transgressing political boundaries of the state. This network found support in states as it furthered the interest of the state through funding and sharing of responsibilities. With the changing times, the distinction between development and corporate investments became blurred. As part of the governance structure, social investment is an important part of doing business. Businesses in order to gain trust among various stakeholders from consumers to community become part of CSR. At present, there has also been a shift from philanthropy to corporate citizenship. Moving towards corporate citizenship could either be seen as bringing all the stakeholders to close proximity and building trust or could be seen as going against free trade. However, CSR also induces competition whereby, benchmarking is a process initiated to review CSR works undertaken by various competitors. The impact of CSR on human society reinstates faith in a product and also in the company resulting in growth in terms of profit. There may not be a single definition of CSR. As a result, increasingly this area of work is broadening thereby including governance issues from sustainable environmental development to protecting the values of human rights (ibid). This may not always be an outcome of a CSR initiative but a consequence of addressing the needs of various stakeholders. For, instance, in the 1980s governments and people have urged the world governments not to carry out business with the repressive regime of South Africa practising Apartheid (ibid).

Corporate Social Responsibility

Corporate Social Responsibility (CSR) is a means by which businesses can benefit the society while managing their own brand. It is a broad concept of corporate citizenship that can take various forms depending on the context of the organization. In the context of family businesses in India, CSR has served as the means to accelerate the need of recognizing corporate citizenship-inducing social accountability for meeting legal, ethical and economic responsibility placed on them by shareholders.

According to The Guardian, the Company Act, 2013 gave birth to legal compliance from the businesses in India. The Act has the following mandate- Under Companies Act, 2013 any company with a (i) net worth of the company to be Rs 500 crore or more or (ii) turnover of the company to be Rs 1000 crore or more or (iii) net profit of the company to be Rs 5 crore or more, has to spend at least 2%of last three years average net profits on CSR activities as specified in Schedule VII and as amended from time to time. The rules came into effect from 1 April 2014. Further, as per the CSR Rules, the provisions of CSR are not only applicable to Indian companies, but also applicable to branch and project offices of a foreign company in India. The qualifying company will be required to constitute a CSR Committee consisting of 3 or more directors. And the CSR Committee shall formulate and recommend to the Board, a policy that indicates the activities to be undertaken, allocates resources and monitor the CSR Policy of the company. If the company did not spend CSR, it has to disclose the reason for not spending. Non-disclosure or absence of the details will be penalized from Rs 50,000 to Rs 25 lakh or even imprisonment of up to three years. India is the first country in the world to enshrine corporate giving into law (The Guardian, 2016). This has led to several benefits. For instance, consumers are socially conscious, many consumers actively seek out companies that support charitable causes. Therefore, CSR attracts customers. CSR also contributes to the competitive advantage as when businesses show how they are more socially responsible than their competitors, they tend to stand out. Lastly, CSR practices have a significant impact on employee morale, as it reinforces her confidence in company's empathy.

But simultaneously with the legislation being enacted, there has been a retreat from the tradition of philanthropy (the family-corporate 'jugalbandi') which emerged from the roots of charity amongst Indian families historically. Now it is just about legal compliance (The Guardian, 2016). The issue of non-compliance is also a source of worry for the system. In a study conducted by Thomas Schmidheiny Centre for Family Enterprise at ISB, the study 'Family Businesses: Heeding the Call of Corporate Conscience, 2015–2017' analyzed the CSR spend behaviour of different categories of firms, based on their ownership structures, for a three-year period from FY 2015 to FY 2017. It has been found out that a greater proportion of family firms met the CSR mandate even as the overall non-compliance level remains a matter of concern. The percentage of family firms that met their CSR obligations or went above the prescribed limit was 50%. The corresponding figure was 45.1% for non-family firms. Family firms are more driven by non-economic utilities and thus more likely to contribute to social welfare activities in keeping with the objective of building an enduring organisation as trustees of society's wealth. However, these firms need to professionalise their social pursuits and build transparent and strong governance mechanisms, the study recommended.

Thus, the way ahead for the country in terms of CSR is to realize that large-scale social innovation. Changes in the system and mandatory spending achieve very little in this direction. It also deflects pressure on companies to change their business practices. CSR should be more inclusive by which an organization should think about and evolve its relationships with stakeholders for the common good and demonstrate its commitment by adopting appropriate business processes and strategies. A set of national voluntary guidelines to spell out what responsible business should look like and set out that CSR is more than just charitable giving should be formalized.

Analysis of the Survey

On conducting a survey with a sample size of 200 respondents, we found out that the awareness amongst the people surrounding CSR is above average. In fact, 83.5% of them have heard of it while 11.5% did not. Although large generalisations cannot be made, yet it can be concluded that the people are starting to be aware of terms like these and their importance, signalling a positive development for the population of the country. There is an increasing agreement in our sample towards the role played by the business groups in contributing to the social welfare of the country. This supports the findings of the ISB study given that more than the business can nurture the expectations of the population (the customers) stronger will be their foundation in the longer run. This is especially true for a family-owned business that needs to secure the future of the organisation. While the business community which contributed the most to social upliftment remains spread out-it also correlates to the context of the survey taker. No concrete conclusion can be truly made regarding the same and depends on the mental programming of the people. But the point that needs consideration in this survey is the realization that business communities must play an important role in the society. But this can be truly realized only when the opaque practices are cut down by them which according to 50% of our sample thinks is the reason why businesses have lost the trust of the citizens of the country. But 36% are not sure and the rest of them doesn't agree. Thus, it is clear that a stable conclusion cannot be drawn from the responses but can be confidently claimed that the realization of the importance of CSR and the role the business communities can play is on a rise amongst the population of the country. In the context of the post globalized world, the survey found out that 58% think that MNCs should be more involved in CSR while 28.5% think that CSR will bring equity in the society. 13.5% think that CSR is just an eyewash. Thus, the scope of CSR to truly influence the social upliftment of the country is still in its initial stage in our country. The good part is how the family business communities are coming forward to uphold the same. This indeed can lead to a greater degree of justice towards the scope of social citizenship and accelerate welfare activities.

References

Bathija, M. (2017) *Paiso: How Sindhis do business*. India: Penguin Random House.

Davis, J.R. and Donald R. (2005) 'Intermediate realms of law: Corporate groups and rulers in Medieval India,' *Journal of the Economic and Social History of the Orient*, 48(1), pp. 92–117.

Drucker, P. (1954) *The practice of management*. US: Harper.

Frederick, R.E. (1999) *Blackwell companions to philosophy: A companion to business ethics*. USA: Blackwell Publishers.

Hatch, J.M. and Cunliffe, A.L. (2006) *Organization theory: Modern, symbolic and postmodern perspectives*. New Delhi: Oxford University Press.

Levi, S.C. (2016) *Caravans: Punjabi Khatri merchants on the silk road*. New Delhi: Penguin Books.

Roy, T. (2018) *A business history of India: Enterprise and emergence of capitalism from 1700*. New Delhi: Cambridge University Press.

Roy, T. (2016) *The East India Company: The world's most powerful corporation*. New Delhi: Portfolio.

Subramanian, L. (2016) *Three merchants of Bombay: Business pioneers of nineteenth century*. India: Random House.

Sundar, P. (2013) *Business and community: A story of corporate social responsibility in India*. New Delhi: Sage Publication.

Timberg, T.A. (2014) *The Marwaris: From Jagat Seth to the Birlas*. New Delhi: Portfolio.

Varoufakis, Y. (2019) *Talking to my daughter: A brief history of capitalism*. London: Vintage.

Weber, M. (2002) *The protestant ethics and the "spirit" of capitalism*. New York: Penguin Books.

6 Does Corporate Citizenship Have Gender?

Amalia Verdu Sanmartin

Introduction

Corporations are required to be accountable for their performance to a variety of different groups including customers, suppliers, employees, governments, and stakeholders. In the construction of this accountability, a responsible image of the corporations materializes in the concept of corporate citizenship. Corporate Citizenship is generally defined as part of the way businesses respond to social responsibilities and indeed become active actors in social change. As part of this, the growing interest in gender equality, to effectively include women and to fight discrimination, should resound in the construction of the corporate citizenship. The interplay between feminist discourse, policies and law have influenced the depiction of the citizen in general, but the extent to which this is reflected in the construct of corporate citizenship remains open for discussion. Historically, the person in law or the citizen has been framed by a normative maleness and the feminist insights unveiled the social construction of the beliefs that view male culture as a norm. This chapter posits that the maleness ascribed to the construct of 'citizen' resounds in the study of corporate citizenship and that further research to explore alternative constructs is required with some urgency. The gendered social construction of citizenship affects the construction of the corporate citizenship as much as it has affected the corporate legal person. Alice Belcher (1997) revealed how the English company law was linked to the maleness of the company. Corporations were male and the characteristics attributed to manhood were expected in the day to day acts. The maleness of the corporation was not only in relation to corporate law but also to the staff gender composition, pay or even to the Board of Directors. The old claim about the maleness of the corporations seems to be something from the past and today transformed into the neutral and inclusive citizen. However, change is generally slow and the male-dominated corporation is present in many areas such as STEM, finance, building, banking. Baxter (2009) refers to the male-dominated corporations like the ones whose culture is sustaining the discourse

DOI: 10.4324/9780429281228-7

about the male as natural born leaders and women as provides support services. This cultural discourse constructs the corporate citizenship as reflected for instance in the staff policies, Board of Directors composition and the corporation policies in general.

The influence of the feminist discourse in law and policies has also affected corporations' policies, strategies, and compositions. The feminist discourse has pushed, within the corporation, an internal movement trying to blur its male roots. Alongside the feminist discourse, the introduction of the concept of gender has become a useful analytical tool to measure the gendered nature of the corporation. Feminism has proposed the use of deconstruction as an effective tool to unveil the gendered aspects of the political subject and can be used to theorize on the gender of the corporate citizenship. This methodology would allow analyzing the hidden gendered aspects within the concept of corporate citizenship.

The male nature of many corporations results in a circumstance that requires organizational culture and social norms to be reconstructed to include a form of corporate citizenship adapted to contemporary needs. There are, of course, many questions that surround this topic. The process of change remains slow and gender equality within corporate environments is, at best, something that continues to develop. The interplay of corporate change with current feminist and gender discourse is likely to influence corporate citizenship, but Gill Coleman (2017) also notes that the corporation through its citizenship has an active role in the reconfiguration of gender.

The extent to which corporations try to become non-male corporation and follow the gender discourse to transform its citizenship varies, of course, adding a further layer of complexity. However, the underlying assumptions concerning this process of transformation should be interrogated as gender can be a slippery concept.

In section 2, we approach the confusion around the concept of corporate citizenship and consider current definitions. In section 3 we approach the interplay of feminist and gender discourses and classify them. In practice, the relation between sex and gender frames the different approaches to the concept of gender. This relationship can be viewed as an alternative between two different approaches: one that views sex as the biological definition and gender as a cultural construct and the alternative viewpoint that understands both sex and gender as cultural constructs. The interplay of these approaches with the feminist discourse leads to different strategies for change. In section 4 we apply the different approaches to gender to the construction of the corporate citizenship to identify different types of corporate citizenship. The feminist discourse on gender has affected the policies and laws that rule corporations and society affecting the chosen corporate citizenship thus their agency in social change (Acker, 2006).

104 *Amalia Verdu Sanmartin*

Defining Corporate Citizenship: Corporate Citizenship and Social Corporate Responsibility

Conceptual confusion regarding corporate citizenship in academia and within the corporations has been a major factor in recent debates. Authors including Matten and Crane (2005) and Gill Coleman (2017) argue for the need for a more theoretical conceptualization of corporate citizenship. A theoretical approach that should be aware of the notions of person, legal person and citizenship and how they intersect with the corporation to produce another abstract active citizen. This changing understanding of corporate citizenship affects the way corporations define themselves which is made accordingly to the kind of citizen they believe to be. This new corporate citizen and the way is designed will define actions, policies and interaction with society and economy. As Maignan and Ferrel (2004) posit, this new citizen is often embraced by those corporations that foresee concrete business benefits, often via marketing.

The CC as a socially active citizen will influence the interaction among all the external and internal stakeholders to the point that it can also trigger significant social changes. Depending on the type of citizen the corporation decides to become will affect how gender relations are configured, achieving a more gender-balanced society or, on the contrary reifying the normative gender roles.

Gender, Sex and the Feminist Discourse

The conceptual debate also exists around the topic of gender, where feminist discourses draw heavily on the discussion around the extent to which both gender and sex are biologically or socially constructed (Louis, 2005; Scott, 1986; Verdu-Sanmartin, 2020). The concept of gender entered into the discourse to distinguish between the culturally constructed and the biologically determined to dismantle fixed gendered roles in society. The modern feminist approach to the concept of gender draws the limits between what must be considered biological and cultural. Sex opposes gender as nature opposes culture thus recognizing a biological sex–sex and a social sex–gender. Sex as part of nature is fixed whereas gender is variable influenced by time and place; Gender is an effect of sex (Valdes, 1995). The critics raised to this approach to the relation between sex and gender resulted in a postmodern approach to gender in which sex is seen as much part of culture as gender. It is not that sex precedes gender but gender precedes sex (Butler, 2011). The outcome is the confusion between sex and gender to enable the existence of gender diversity. The boundaries between sex and gender become blurrier; Sex is an effect of gender.

To understand how these two approaches depict the subject differently and accordingly the corporate citizenship is the Negri and Hardt's opinion about the difference between modern and postmodern thought:

"[W]hat really divides them is that modernists want to protect or resurrect the traditional social bodies and postmodernists accept or even celebrate their dissolution" (Hardt and Negri, 2004, p. 190). Besides the division between modern and postmodern theories of gender, Lorber's classification of the different feminist epistemologies by their approach to the concept of gender as Gender balance, Gender Resistance and Gender Rebellion is extremely useful (Lorber, 2010). A combination of both, the use of the concept of gender and Lorber feminist classification serves as the framework to elaborate my own classification and by parallelism deconstruct-reconstruct the corporate citizenship.

The debate is summarized here as Table 6.1:

The brief classification made by Gill Coleman specify four different stages in feminism that can be related to the changing status of women in corporations (Coleman, 2017). These four stages can be combined with the feminist approach to gender to understand the role of gender in constructing the corporate citizenship. A more complex classification in which the relation between sex and gender takes the main role also allows us to visualize how legal changes and policies interplay with corporations influencing the type of corporate citizenship.

Feminism, Gender and the Corporate Citizenship

The initial subject grounding the corporate citizenships is the modern Cartesian person, the male with body and reason that is able to take decisions and act in society. The corporation, as aforementioned, was recognized as a male Cartesian person acting in society and affecting the path of economics and politics. But, who is the corporate citizen now?

The feminist discourse on sex and gender influence law and policies but we do not know to what extend it has influenced the corporations. Sex and gender have been approached from very different perspectives and how these perspectives influence the corporation brings some light on the type of citizen corporations have become. Looking at the composition of the Boards of Directors and the staff distribution shows the lack of diversity and evidences of how corporations tend to speak with a male single voice and, sometimes with a female choir. The influence of the different approaches to sex and gender have affected the depiction of the legal person. The original modern person is depicted as stable, coherent, self-conscious, rational, autonomous, and universal 'reasonable man'. This person gives meaning to the world through reason. The postmodern approach to gender however depicts a connected and relational being uniquely created by experiences.

Gender reform feminism tries as Gill Coleman defines 'Equip the Woman' aiming to eliminate formal, educational, and political inequalities. It is restricted to the inclusion of women in the public realm following male standards. It is the assimilation of women into the public

Table 6.1 Summary of the debate

Approach	Relation	Feminism	Corporation	Coleman	Citizen
Modern	Sex vs gender	Gender Reform Gender Resistance	C – MALE C- Male	Stage one: "Equip the woman" Stage two: "Create Equal Opportunities" Stage three: "Value difference"	Modern person
Post-Modern	Sex/gender	Gender Rebellion Gender Revolution	C- Male/Female Degendered/Desexed	Stage four: Resisting dominant discourse -----------------------	Postmodern person

Does Corporate Citizenship Have Gender? 107

realm giving them the opportunity of embracing male standards. The search for formal equality focuses on offering training, education, and support to women to enable them to move into more senior organizational positions (Coleman, 2017). The measures affect the public realm leaving the private untouched without addressing the women's responsibilities that constraint their access to senior positions. The corporate citizenship is a male citizen that imposes its standards and perspective as the norm. Women can be in the public realm under the rule of men. Women enter corporations by assuming "helpers' roles while still neglected from the leader ones. The minority of women who climb up to the senior positions with responsibility need to adopt normative male standards and requires women to do all the work to overcome their perceived 'disadvantage' (Coleman, 2017). Women are the gender, and they need to prove that gender is a cultural construction as their sex still leads its possibilities.

Feminist legal strategies highlight the absence of women in corporations and oblige them to make the necessary changes into law to accept formal equality. There is an "adequate similarity", rather than equality that does not affect the depiction of the corporate citizen (Evans, 1995, p. 13). This is evidenced enacting an equal pay policy which still is not achieved in many corporations as described for example in the annual gender pay gap report of national states. The corporate citizenship is the abstract, universal modern subject of law represented by the Cartesian person with a male body. The materiality of the body intra-act with every other element of society, law, politics and corporations legitimizing the male body as the universal.

Gender Resistance feminism refers to cultural, radical, psychoanalytic, French difference, Marxist/Socialist feminisms among many others, an amalgam of feminism whose shared point lies in their focus on power and how it creates a hierarchy in which the feminine is devalued. Women are in a disadvantaged position because of the normative sex hierarchy. Gender is separated from sex and mainstreamed by power. Gender is the imposition of certain cultural beliefs (patriarchal beliefs, structures, norms) on sex. Masculine culture is the norm, and women should create a feminine culture defined by themselves. Women need to resist gender while revaluing their specific nature.

The focus is on equity rather than on equality. Equality needs to be redefined to include the natural differences. The culture of care, nurture, needs to become part of the public space. Sexuality is is a central place of oppression kept within the private space. Sexuality establishes the functioning of the social structures of reproduction, sex, socialization of children that enable men to control women (Evans, 1995; Mitchell, 1974).

Feminine values and experiences need to become part of the public space and be incorporated into law. The aim is to value the feminine rather than embracing male standards. The male corporation should

108 *Amalia Verdu Sanmartin*

recognize the value of the feminine which might entail a significant shift in the depiction of corporate citizenship. The lack of feminine perspective results, as Coleman (2017) explains, in biased recruitment, selection, and promotion techniques besides gender segregation of workplaces and occupations. The recognition of the specificities of the women experience will unveil the constraints imposed on them in the private sphere that affects their performance in the public space. This is the place for most women's responsibilities and corporations need to acknowledge women differences in their corporate policies. The inclusion of women as women into the corporation influences the feminisation of corporations including maternal and pregnancy leaves, children related measures and measures against sexual harassment. The inclusion of women experiences entails the recognition of sexual harassment in the corporation together with motherhood and children related measures that oblige to acknowledge the differences between women and men in terms of needs and experiences. Nevertheless, still, this approach does not allow for a total inclusion of women into corporations or the achievement of a positive degendered corporate citizenship because the woman responsibilities are acknowledged but not shared (Nousiainen *et al.*, 2018).

Deconstruct the universal subject envisage the reconstruction of a new universal subject tainted with feminine traits. The universal subject includes all feminine values. The feminine essence becomes revalued thus women's sexuality, motherhood and children related responsibilities are feminine and, as such, incorporated in law. Nevertheless, the understanding of the feminine nature still relies on the normative belief about the meaning of woman and womanhood defined by men. The male corporate citizenship framework dictates what women needs and experiences are and, as such, reflected in workplace policies. We might say that corporation becomes "pregnant with meaning" (Lacey, 1997, p. 65). The feminine nature implicitly embedded in all women obviates those who do not identify with this feminine essence. The gender resistance approach fosters the inclusion of parental leave and flexible working to allow women to care for their feminine responsibilities. These measures mean that women must follow the dictates of the feminine essence assuming they are a homogeneous group and denying the existence of women who would not need these measures or, who would prefer to share these responsibilities with their partners. This approach reifies the maleness of the corporation by assuming these measures are for women keeping in place the unconscious boundaries between the public and the private. The reconstruction of the subject is two modern Cartesian subjects: the male and the female. The male is located in the public realm and the female in both the public and the private realms.

CC has now some feminine traits, those keeping women in their feminine role and reifying the normative gender roles. Dualism helps to "do gender" – The male and female genders are embedded in social structures, and therefore men also "do" gender through their gendered behaviour towards women and other men. Corporate citizenship as a male with privileges do gender and replicate this process by adjusting their behaviour to make it consistent with what society expects from their sex within the male-female dichotomy. Gender reproduces itself through corporate citizenship discourse. It is what Butler describes as the performance of gender. Society is a place where gender reinstates through our performance and behaviour, which accord with an internalized notion of gender norms and the corporate citizenship designed by gender resistance takes a role in the performance of gender. The corporation creates gender involuntarily through "regulative discourses" that control our way of behaving and construct sex.

Gender Rebellion refers to postmodern feminism, all the post- movements (post-structuralist, postmodern, post-feminism) and masculinities. Their approach to the relation between sex and gender is postmodern, meaning that both gender and sex are culturally constructed. Gender rebellion envisages difference from a broader perspective, becoming 'the generation of complex identities' (Chamallas, 1999, p. 15). Diversity has become a core concept, although within the boundaries imposed by the binary of sex/genders. Sexual orientation, ethnicity, nationality, age etc.. become another determining factor of identity, justifying the existence of many identities within every sex group. Intersectionality is at the core of identity-making, challenging the homogeneity of the group.

The postmodern subject tries to find its place. Still, it cannot overcome the myth of the modern unitary subject framework – the truth of the modern subjects hinders the possibilities of a postmodern subject made of multiple truths. The evident diversity among women and men gets trapped within the truth of the discursive woman and man. The binary of sex limits the materialization of the body, and biology continues to rule gender. There is challenging sex essentialism to overcome, law and policies only reflect the truth of the discursive biology of sex. On the bright side, broadening the group's heterogeneity blurs the strict boundaries between man and woman. The feminine policies to include women experiences and children responsibilities will now incorporate those men who do not feel ashamed of sharing feminine responsibilities. The group's heterogeneity becomes evident when dissolving heteronormativity of sexuality, obliging to transform policies to include same-sex families and single parenthood.

Gender rebellion finds a way to shake the most conservative institution that of marriage, recognizing same-sex marriage in many legal systems. It also forces to include sexual orientation as one of the grounds for discrimination alongside sex and gender. The female responsibilities regarding motherhood and children start to be legally shared with the male sex, although still not under the same conditions. However, these legal measures leave room for the corporation to improve them through their specific policies and the way they relate with other actors. The corporate

110 *Amalia Verdu Sanmartin*

citizenship can be constructed differently and expand the limits imposed by gender. The acceptation of sex and gender as culture allows to denaturalize sex rights and responsibilities and foresees the possibility of androgynous corporate citizenship.

The citizen is an androgynous person with masculine and feminine traits. Corporate citizenship becomes fluid and sex, and gender discrimination becomes a core issue in policies and strategies. Corporate citizenship is tolerant of sex and sexual orientation and, as such, the internal and external relations of the corporation with the different actors. Nevertheless, gender rebellion feminism, as Toril Moi claims "[w]ith respect to sex and gender poststructuralists are reformist rather than revolutionary" (Moi, 2001, p. 4). The revolution still is to come.

Gender Revolution is not a paradigm used by Lorber's classification. The gender revolution is the natural continuation of gender rebellion which represents the transition from modern to postmodern while gender revolution is already looking at the postmodern person. It is a step forward in the postmodern approach to gender. Sex is culture as much as gender. Gender revolution rejects the normative binary opposition of masculine/feminine. This approach represents a big turn from the previous movements, questions about female discrimination and oppression are no longer the focus of attention. They rebelled against the normative sexual and gender identities characterized by the masculine and feminine frameworks.

The position represented by gender revolution confronts that of the other movements. Gender reform, gender resistance, and gender rebellion all restrict themselves to the limits of the category woman and the duality imposed by normative sex/gender. The category woman is blurred, and the aim is to question discursive categories and focus on the outlaws not fitting on limits imposed by the legitimized truth. The elimination of the actual subject tries to shed light on the cultural construction of the categories sex and gender, moving towards the destruction of the subject as we know it and in the blurring of boundaries. The citizen escapes the limitations imposed by the normative and constructs a universal abstract subject able to choose independently of its sex or gender freely. Gender revolution shows how a sexed one has replaced the universal subject. A sexed legal subject constructed within the natural binary and transposed to society as the universal citizen. Accepting the postmodern approach to gender entails queering the law and the subject, consequently the queering of the citizen. The postmodern subject is, however, rather a utopian dream which hardly resounds in law or the political realm (Otto, 2017).

The deconstruction of the subject unveils the male normative standards that constitute the citizen as we know it. According to Golder (2004), deconstruction has revealed tensions as using deconstructive strategies requires a reconstruction adapted to the modern discourse.

The possibilities of reconstruction then are constrained by the imposition of the modern framework, thus hindering the potential of a reconstructive project towards a postmodern subject. Diversity poorly recognizes male and female heterogeneity keeping norms and policies within the binary, showing the difficulties in constructing a real inclusive corporate citizenship when the reconstruction follows a male understanding or even a feminist understanding of women and gender.

The reconstruction of the citizen happens within the limits of the binary of sex. Gender reform and gender resistance reconstruct a male citizen to some extent acknowledging the feminine essence. The latter recognises the existence of women as women in the private realm. Gender rebellion constructs a 60% male and 40% woman pushing society to achieve a desired 50/50. Then gender revolution destroys sex and gender, allowing freedom without imposing any trait or characteristic, which in the end are all gendered.

Constructing the Citizen of the Corporate Citizenship

The feminist use of deconstruction envisages a reconstructive strategy to tackle the negative and discriminatory gendered performances that are also embedded within the corporate citizenship. The reconstructive project within feminism, as described by Calhoun has two stages, one "to reconstruct the category 'woman'" by redefining, rejecting, and revaluing the feminine traits. Second, "reconstructing the category 'woman' represented within feminism itself" (Calhoun and Benhabib, 1994, p. 8). The result however does not expand beyond diversity and continue imposing norms of conduct. Being outside of these norms of conduct implies becoming a minority. Therefore, the corporation when transposing these discourses reproduces the same mistakes and reifies the normative roles.

Calhoun pinpoints two shared aspects among different feminist movements framing the process of deconstruction –reconstruction: 1) gender as the leading cause of oppression, and 2) reconstruction to obtain a non-discriminated subject (Calhoun and Benhabib, 1994). These two aspects also might apply to the process of deconstruction – construction of the corporate citizenship as gender understood as the cultural construct takes a significant role for corporations, for instance, highlighting the lack of women and the need to reconstruct genderless corporate citizenship.

There is a direct link between legal changes, policies, and corporate citizenship influenced by the feminist discourse. There is a common subject for all of them to whom address their policies, laws, and discourses. This person is the social, legal and political citizen who is also the model for corporate citizenship. The feminist deconstruction of the subject focuses on identity and power hierarchies to understand the effect of sex and gender. It allows understanding the impact on laws and policies and being aware of the agency of an abstract entity such as corporate citizenship.

112 *Amalia Verdu Sanmartin*

The agency of the corporate agency resounds inside and outside of the corporation becomes an active agent of change. The corporations follow the socio-political discourses and adapt to become what is considered a good citizen. Their choice is crucial because it has a significant effect on the way the world is understood. Corporate citizenship has agency. Corporate citizenship means becoming an active citizen and goes beyond a mere image of the corporation. Being a socially engaged citizen implies setting the corporation's accepted behaviour that affects how it relates to others, leading performance inside and outside the corporations. Corporate citizenship has the power of influencing the whole social system because it is part of it, relates to it and even decide on it.

References

Acker, J. (2006) 'Gender and organizations'. *Handbook of the sociology of gender.* US: Springer, pp. 177–194.

Baxter, J. (2009) *The language of female leadership, the language of female leadership.* Basingstoke: Palgrave Macmillan.

Belcher, A. (1997) 'Gendered company: Views of corporate governance at the institute of directors', *Feminist Legal Studies,* 5(1), pp. 57–76.

Butler, J. (2011) *Gender trouble: Feminism and the subversion of identity.* London: Routledge.

Calhoun, C. and Benhabib, S. (1994) 'Situating the self: Gender, community, and postmodernism in contemporary ethics', *The Journal of Philosophy,* 91(8), p. 426.

Chamallas, M. (1999) *Introduction to feminist legal theory.* Colorado: Aspen Law & Business.

Coleman, G. (2017) 'Gender, power and post-structuralism in corporate citizenship: A personal perspective on theory and change', *Globalization and corporate citizenship: The alternative gaze: A collection of seminal essays,* 5, pp. 224–235.

Evans, J.A. (1995) *Feminist theory today: An introduction to second-wave feminism.* New York: Sage Publications.

Golder, B. (2004) 'Rethinking the subject of postmodern feminist legal theory: Towards a feminist foucaultian jurisprudence', *Southern Cross University Law Review,* 8, pp. 73.

Hardt, M. and Negri, A. (2004) *Multitude: War and democracy in the age of empire.* London: The Penguin Press.

Lacey, N. (1997) 'On the subject of sexing the subject', in Ngaire N. and Owens R.J. (eds.), *Sexing the Subject.* North Ryde.

Lorber, J. (2010) *Gender Inequality: Feminist theories and politics,* 4th edn. Oxford, New York: Oxford University Press.

Louis, M.-V. (2005) 'Tell me, what does 'gender' really mean?', *Sisyphe,* available at: http://www.marievictoirelouis.net/document.php?id=737&themeid=877.

Maignan, I. and Ferrel, O. (2004) 'Corporate social responsibility and marketing: An integrative framework', *Journal of the Academy of Marketing Science,* 32(1), pp. 3–19.

Matten, D. and Crane, A. (2005) 'Note coporate citizenship: Toward and extended theorethical conceptualization', *Management Review*, 30, pp. 166–179.

Mitchell, J. (1974) *Psychoanalysis and feminism*. New York: Pantheon Books.

Moi, T. (2001) *What is a woman?: And other essays*. Oxford: Oxford University Press.

Nousiainen, K., Gunnarsson, A., Lundstrom, K. and Niemi-Kiesilainen, J. (eds.). (2018), *Responsible Selves*, 1st ed., 20.

Otto, D. (2017) *Queering international law: Possibilities, alliances, complicities, risks*, Taylor and Francis, July 14th 2017.

Scott, J.W. (1986) 'Gender: A useful category of historical analysis', *The American Historical Review*, 91(5), pp. 1053–1075.

Valdes, F. (1995) 'Queers, sissies, dykes, and tomboys: Deconstructing the conflation of sex,gender and sexual orientation', *California Law Review*, 83(1), p. 3.

Verdu-Sanmartin, A. (2020) *Trapped in gender: Understanding the concept of gender and its use in law*. Turku, Finland: Univeristy of Turku.

7 Impact of Financial and Cost Management Systems for Family-Owned Businesses' Corporate Citizenship

Padmi Nagirikandalage and Arnaz Binsardi

Introduction

Family-owned businesses have been linked with corporate citizenship (Carrigan and Buckley, 2008; Kashmiri and Mahajan, 2010) where businesses attempt to meet the economic, legal, social and ethical responsibilities. This could be due to stakeholder pressure on them (Maignan and Ferrell, 2000) and also due to the reputation of the businesses which leads them to act as good corporate citizens (Miller *et al.*, 2008). Since corporate citizenship has been used interchangeably with corporate social responsibility (CSR) (Matten and Crane, 2005), corporate citizenship also could be referred to as the relationships between a business and social, ethical, and environmental issues (Birch, 2011) like CSR. Due to maintaining such healthy relationships, family-owned businesses could enhance their reputation as well (Sharma and Manikutty, 2005). Hence, family-owned businesses would drive towards being good corporate citizens as well.

Moreover, due to the involvement of family, the objectives of such businesses could represent both family and business entity oriented objectives together (Chrisman *et al.*, 2012; Dyer and Whetten, 2006; Olson *et al.*, 2003; Whetten and Mackey, 2005; Zellweger *et al.*, 2013). These objectives could be either financial or non-financial (Dyer and Whetten, 2006; Gómez-Mejía *et al.*, 2007) where the financial benefit is expected mainly or not respectively. However, family-owned businesses have not been vastly discussed along with financial management systems in order to create freedom to engage in the corporate citizenship agenda (Binz *et al.*, 2017; Seaman, 2017) although some literature is evident in non-financial objectives with family-owned businesses (Zellweger *et al.*, 2013). Moreover, the corporate models have been widely discussed, hence it dominates the literature (Gersick *et al.*, 1997; Litz, 1997). The reason behind this could be due to the fact that family-owned businesses have been perceived differently as they have not been emphasised significantly in the field of entrepreneurship as well (Donckels and Fröhlich, 1991). Hence, the theoretical and empirical research is still at an infancy level where the doors are open to research on family-owned businesses further.

DOI: 10.4324/9780429281228-8

Additionally, family-owned businesses have contributed largely to a country's economy (Poutziouris, Steier, and Smyrnios, 2004). This could be due to the fact that the corporate citizenship recognises that an organisation has social, cultural and environmental responsibilities to the community in which it operates as well as economic and financial responsibilities to its shareholders and stakeholders as well. However, as per these responsibilities and for family-owned businesses, it could be difficult to accomplish mostly due to their lack of financial robustness. Hence, it is vital to explore the barriers or hindrances that may lead to prevent family-owned businesses to engage fully with the corporate citizenship agenda. Moreover, this paper investigates the ways and means of implementing sound financial and cost management systems in family-owned businesses and how it could support these businesses to have the freedom to engage fully in the corporate citizenship agenda.

Furthermore, this paper focuses on family-owned businesses operating in an emerging economy as the hindrances that any family-owned business meets may vary compared to operating in a developed economy. Since the post-war developments are booming with foreign investments and being a culturally distinct within the South Asian region, family-owned businesses operating within Sri Lanka has been considered for this research study. Moreover, as an emerging economy, the Sri Lankan context has also shown similar statistics for family-owned businesses. The family-owned businesses in Sri Lanka represent a majority of the micro-businesses (1–4 employees) and Small and Medium Enterprises (SMEs) where small (5- 25 employees) and medium (26–100) size organisations (Department of census and statistics, 2015). Although, the contribution to the country's economy is significant as such, there are various issues and hindrances that the family-owned businesses are facing locally and internationally. Amongst them, issues and hindrances around financial and cost management in family-owned businesses play a significant role in increasing their economic performance and sustainability.

Moreover, having an effective financial and cost management system is a prerequisite of a responsible business to its community. As an effective financial and cost management system is considered, they play a significant role where maintaining an efficient and effective financial and cost management system could benefit these businesses vastly in order to face the local as well as global challenges and risks in the future. A financial and cost management system is a systematic framework used by a firm to estimate the finances and cost of their products for measuring their profitability (Bragg, 2001; Drury, 2015; Martin, 2014; Obara and Ukpai, 2001; Romney and Steinbart, 2011). Financial and cost management systems include the simple cost of goods sold and an inventory valuation, a breakeven analysis, a full and variable costing analysis, variance analysis (VA) and activity-based costing (ABC) (Nagirikandalage and Binsardi, 2017). Previous literature (Hansen *et al.*, 2009; Kwan, 2011) indicates

116 *Padmi Nagirikandalage and Arnaz Binsardi*

that companies efficiently use financial and cost management systems outperform, in terms of their global competitiveness, those which do not. Moreover, an effective cost accounting system could improve the small businesses' financial management as well.

The purpose of this paper is to critically explore the impact of financial and cost management systems (CAS) on family-owned businesses in terms of enhancing an effective financial management while increasing their performances in order to engage fully in the corporate citizenship agenda. In particular, it aims to explore the financial and cost management system of these family-owned businesses while examining the impact of changing dynamics and Sri Lankan cultural and local characteristics on the adoption of financial and cost management systems. This will help to identify the impact on enhancing the performance of a business and to evaluate its impact on the engagement of the corporate citizenship agenda as well. In particular, it examines the factors that facilitate or hinder the usage of an effective and efficient financial and cost management systems in family-owned businesses as a case in Sri Lanka.

This research is invaluable as a tool not only for Sri Lankan policymakers but also for wider prospects and practitioners, to enable the usage of sound financial and cost management systems in order to enhance family-owned businesses performances both financially and non-financially while engaging in the corporate citizenship agenda. As well as policymakers and practitioners, this research could be employed by academicians for advancing theoretical development around the change and cultural triggers and barriers for adopting more innovative and fresher financial and cost management system in order to encourage family-owned businesses' engagement in corporate citizenship agenda. This chapter has been presented with an introduction including the background for this study. The methodology, findings and discussion will follow consecutively and finally with a conclusion.

Methodology

Primary data for the research was obtained by interviewing selected respondents from Sri Lanka's family-owned businesses in manufacturing sector. They were selected using purposeful as this method allows researchers to understand how a phenomenon is seen and understood among different people, in different settings and at different times. Also, here, the maximum variation sampling method (MVS) is employed to meet a maximum diverse group to get a deeper, and overall picture of the peoples' perception with regarding the use of a cost system to optimise the purpose of corporate citizenship. A total of 5 respondents were interviewed, which resulted and several theories being employed to analyse them within the corporate citizenship.

Findings and Discussion

The findings of this research were based on primary data, which were collected through in-depth interviews with selected respondents. A case study has been carried out which was selected through purposive sampling to capture issues related to the phenomena of triggers and barriers to adopting the financial and cost management systems within a family-owned business in Sri Lanka. The selected respondents originated from the manufacturing sector specialised in coconut related productions in the North West region of the country.

Furthermore, since the thematic analysis was adopted in this study, the analysis has been carried out according to the themes identified by Altman and Vidaver-Cohen (2000). The triple bottom line approach (Norman and MacDonald, 2004) also emphasises the engagement with society and performance objectives of the business as some of the leading forces for corporate citizenship activities. The findings also align with this as per the respondents mentioned;

> '...we do engage with the society in several ways...for example in the village we operate we have identified some schools who are under privileged and as our raw materials mainly come from coconut trees we distribute coconut plants to these schools for free. So they can plant them in their schools and later we can buy them from them so the school can use that money for improvements of facilities in the school...' (R1)

> '...the hospital chairman of our village hospital usually inform a list of required machines, etc. if the government funds are not enough to cover those costs. So we donate these machines, etc. with our capacity to do so. We have been doing this for so long, so the hospital even knows our employees and when they admit to the hospital they specially look after them as a gratitude of what we have been doing as a company...' (R2)

These findings imply the fact that how engagement with society could benefit especially from the aspects of non-financial performance of the family-owned business. For example, as mentioned by the respondent, their employees could benefit from health service due to family-owned business's engagement in improving the quality of life of the villagers by donating to the village hospital. This could lead to employees' loyalty towards the business and in turn, this could improve the family-owned business performance with an efficient staff or labour.

However, the family-owned business could have been able to invest in such activities due to a proper management of their finances and costing as well.

118   *Padmi Nagirikandalage and Arnaz Binsardi*

'...we monitor our cash flows monthly...so we have a better understanding of our outgoings and profit and it has helped us to budget our activities very well and it shows the surplus cash within the business that we could use to donate to schools, hospitals, etc. in the village...' (R3) (Owner, Coconut production Company)

Theme 2: Global Corporate Citizenship

This theme relates to linking citizenship practice with industry distinctions where family-owned business management is encouraged to observe and address the global issues but may apply in the local context as well. Hence, to accomplish the corporate citizenship agenda, family-owned businesses are required to predict such challenges and transform their businesses to meet these challenges effectively and efficiently.

As the findings show below, the local family-owned business but being an exporter as well may need to meet global trade requirements especially on ethical aspects and other global challenges such as climate change issues. Therefore, the businesses are expected to invest largely in environmental friendly waste management systems and other methods to go along with the global trade.

'...as we export our organic products to other countries we have to follow certain guidelines in terms of waste management, production, etc. So we have obtained ISO as a requirement and therefore we need to pay more attention on our day to day production should be careful on waste handling with the environment. So our financial and cost management system has helped us a lot to find money needed to manage our waste. As you know we have to take our waste to a given place by the local council on our own cost, we need to find an environmental friendly way to destroy these...so we have to find money within our business and our cost management system has helped us so far to achieve this...' (R4)

Therefore, the about finding also shows that financial and cost management systems could assist in finding the required funds for the investments required within the family-owned business and in turn meeting the global corporate citizenship goals as well.

Theme 3: Stakeholder Relationship

As per Waddock and Smith (2000), citizenship implies the 'social' aspects of overall corporate responsibility. Hence, in addition to the above findings R1 and R2, the following quotes of a respondent also imply the fact that how the family-owned business es not only engage but also perceive the social aspects as the businesses' responsibility.

'...most of our employees are old women. Also, their children may live far away as they do not live with them anymore and majority of these old women are low income villagers too. So they may need more money for health issues such as serious operations, etc. But they can claim some money from the presidential fund in Sri Lanka according to their low income, and we pay the rest of hospital bills as well as any immediate family members of them as we treat all of them as one big family and consider it as our responsibility look after the elderly villagers...our thinking has helped us to establish strongly and has lasted long within the village so far...' (R5)

Theme 4: Transformation

The combination of commercial and social forces driving the business to change toward improved citizenship. As per the findings also indicate that the family-owned businesses to transform their systems in order to meet the social responsibilities. For example, the respondents have mentioned that the introduction of new internal auditing structure and a financial and cost management and budgeting system have reinforced meeting the goals of the business with improved performance and in turn has assisted the corporate citizenship agenda as well.

Theme 5: Business Opportunity

As per Fombrun (1996, 1997), the citizenship activities can promote strategic goals of the business has been further established in the findings of this study as the respondents' mentioned;

'...we were expected to donate to the religious places and also to the local council and the police facilities as they got to know how we have been donating to the village hospital...since we have been doing such activities to improve the quality life in the village society, we were sub contracted to provide another services to the school and the police as well...we distributed plant to the school and they could get the help of the students and staff and maintain a small plantation in the school and we could but those raw materials for a cheaper price later as we initiated the project with the help from the local council...'

Theme 6: Partnership Society

It has been perceived that all sectors including, private, public and society must work together in a mutually beneficial and strategically driven manner (Altman and Vidaver-Cohen, 2000). The findings have been aligned with this

120 Padmi Nagirikandalage and Arnaz Binsardi

as the respondents mentioned that maintaining a good relationship with the local council has benefitted them to resolve some environmental regulatory matters such as finding a suitable place for waste management taxation, etc. Also, due to the benefits received by the society as per R1, R2, R3 it could be argued the fact that the employees who are part of the society being satisfied with the benefits they receive from the business may lead to having an efficient workforce for the business to achieve the goals successfully.

However, the above discussion in various themes implies the fact that a business should maintain their financial and cost management at a satisfactory level in order to meet their social and financial responsibilities, hence the need for a financial and cost management system in terms of maintaining a corporate citizenship agenda within a family-owned business.

Conclusion

This study explores the adoption of financial and cost management systems in order to evaluate the impact on enhancing the performance of a business and to evaluate its impact on the engagement of the corporate citizenship agenda using the qualitative case study research approach. As qualitative research is used, the limitation of the study is that the knowledge produced might not be generalisable to other countries or other industries.

The research found that the family-owned businesses have been adopting financial and cost management systems in order to improve the business performance as well as aligned with the corporate citizenship agenda. However, other factors such as lack of funds available for investment and cost management are considered as barriers to the implementation of required systems within family-owned businesses. This study is expected to guide further theoretical development in the area of corporate citizenship especially for developing economies as well. For example, by combining financial and cost management systems with the aspects of imperfect technology and limited industrialisation, innovative systems can be designed for developing economies. Moreover, this paper is invaluable for practitioners and policymakers in facilitating the adoption of more modern financial and cost management systems to enhance the industry's competitive advantage. That is, with proper systems implementations in the future, family-owned businesses could benefit from strengthening the trade relations with other Southeast Asian countries and beyond.

References

Altman, B. and Vidaver-Cohen, D. (2000), 'A framework for understanding corporate citizenship', *Business and Society Review*, 105, pp. 1–7.
Binz, C.A. *et al.* (2017) 'Family business goals, corporate citizenship behaviour and firm performance: disentangling the connections', *International Journal of Management and Enterprise Development*, 16, (1/2), pp. 34–56.

Financial and Cost Management Systems   121

Birch, D. (2011) 'Corporate citizenship: Rethinking business beyond corporate social responsibility', *Perspectives on Corporate Citizenship*, pp. 53–65.

Bragg, S.M. (2001), *Cost accounting: A comprehensive guide*, Hardcover ed., New York, NY: John Wiley and Sons.

Carrigan, M. and Buckley, J. (2008) 'What's so special about family business? An exploratory study of UK and Irish consumer experiences of family businesses', *International Journal of Consumer Studies*, 32(6), pp. 656–666.

Chrisman, J.J., Chua, J.H. and Steier, L. (2005). 'Sources and consequences of distinctive familiness: An introduction', *Entrepreneurship Theory and Practice*, 29(3), pp. 237–247. 10.1111/j.1540-6520.2005.00080.x

Chrisman, J.J. *et al.* (2012) 'Family involvement, family influence, and family-centered non-economic goals in small firms', *Entrepreneurship Theory and Practice*, 36(2), pp. 267–293.

Donckels, R. and Fröhlich, E. (1991) 'Are family owned business es really different? European experiences from STRATOS', *Family Owned Business Review*, 4(2), pp. 149–160. 10.1111/j.1741-6248.1991.00149.x

Drury, C. (2015) *Management and cost accounting*, Paperback, 9th ed., London: Cengage Learning, ISBN-10: 1408093936.

Dyer, W.G. and Whetten, D.A. (2006) 'Family firms and social responsibility: Preliminary evidence from the S&P 500', *Entrepreneurship Theory and Practice*, 30(6), pp. 785–802.

Fombrun, C.J. (1996) *Reputation: Realizing value from the corporate image.* Boston: Harvard Business School Press.

Fombrun, C.J. 1997. 'Three elements of corporate citizenship: Ethics, social benefit, and profitability', in Tichy N.M., McGill A.R., and Clair L. St. (eds.), *Corporate citizenship: Doing business in the public eye.* San Francisco: New Lexington Press, pp. 27–42.

Gersick, K.E. *et al.* 1997) *Generation to generation: Life cycle of the family owned business.* Boston: Harvard Business School Press.

Gómez-Mejía, L.R. *et al.* (2007) 'Socioemotional wealth and business risks in family-controlled firms: evidence from Spanish olive oil mills', *Administrative Science Quarterly*, 52(1), pp. 106–137.

Hansen, D.R., Guan, L. and Mowen, M.M. (2009) *Cost management.* Mason, OH: South-Western Cengage Learning. 10.1111/j.1741-6248.1988.00427.x

Kashmiri, S. and Mahajan, V. (2010) 'What's in a name? An analysis of the strategic behaviour of family firms', *International Journal of Research in Marketing*, 27(3), pp. 271–280.

Kwan, L.H. (2011) 'Competing globally with cost accounting', University of Tennessee Honors Thesis Projects, available at: http://trace.tennessee.edu/utk_chanhonoproj/1429

Litz, R.A. (1997). 'The family firm's exclusion from business school research: Explaining the void; addressing the opportunity'. *Entrepreneurship Theory and Practice*, 21(3), pp. 55–71. 10.1177/104225879702100304

Maignan, I. and Ferrell, O.C. (2000) *Journal of Business Ethics*, 23, 283. https://doi-org.manchester.idm.oclc.org/10.1023/A:1006262325211

Maignan, I., Ferrell, O.C. and Hult, G.T.M.J. (1999) 'Corporate citizenship: Cultural antecedents and business benefits', *Journal of the Academy of Marketing Science*, 27(4), pp. 455–469. https://doi-org.manchester.idm.oclc.org/10.1177/0092070399274005

Martin, J.R. (2014), *Management Accounting: Concepts, Techniques and Controversial Issues*, Management and Accounting Web, available at: http://maaw.info/MAAWTextbookMain.htm

Matten, D. and Crane, A. (2005) 'Corporate citizenship: Toward an extended theoretical conceptualization', *Academy of Management Review*, 30(1), pp. 166–179.

Miller, D., Le Breton-Miller, I. and Scholnick, B. (2008) 'Stewardship vs. stagnation: an empirical comparison of small family and non-family businesses', *Journal of Management Studies*, 45(1), pp. 51–78.

Nagirikandalage, P. and Binsardi, B. (2017). 'Inquiry into the cultural impact on cost accounting systems (CAS) in Sri Lanka', *Managerial Auditing Journal*, 32, pp. 463–499. 10.1108/MAJ-02-2016-1313.

Norman, W. and MacDonald, C., (2004), 'Getting to the bottom of "Triple Bottom Line"', *Business Ethics Quarterly*, 14(2), pp. 243–262.

Obara, L.C. and Ukpai, N.A. (2001), 'Cost accounting practice in the informal sector of Nigeria (a survey of eastern business zone)', *African Administrative Studies*, 56, pp. 91–102.

Olson, P.D. *et al.* (2003) 'The impact of the family and the business on family business sustainability', *Journal of Business Venturing*, 18(5), pp. 639–666.

Poutziouris, P., Steier, L., and Smyrnios, K. (2004), 'A commentary on family business entrepreneurial developments', *International Journal of Entrepreneurial Behaviour & Research*, 10(2), pp. 7–11.

Romney, M.B. and Steinbart, P.J. (2011), *Accounting information systems*, 12th International ed., Upper River Saddle, NJ: Prentice Hall, ISBN-10: 0273754378.

Seaman, C., 2017. 'Turning point: Factoring the family into corporate citizenship', *J. Corp. Citizsh*, 65, pp. 6e11. 10.9774/GLEAF.4700.2017.ma.00003.

Sharma, P. and Manikutty, S. (2005), 'Strategic divestments in family firms: Role of family structure and community culture', *Entrepreneurship Theory and Practice*, 29(3), pp. 293–311.

Waddock, S. and Smith, N. (2000) 'Relationships: The real challenge of corporate global citizenship', *Business and Society Review*, 105, pp. 47–62.

Whetten, D. and Mackey, A. (2005) *An identity-congruence explanation of why firms would consistently engage in corporate social performance*, Working paper. Provo, UT: Brigham Young University.

Zellweger, T.M. *et al.* (2013) 'Why do family firms strive for nonfinancial goals? An organizational identity perspective', *Entrepreneurship Theory and Practice*, 37(2), pp. 229–248.

8 Consciously Contributing: Community Engagement, Philanthropy and Family Business

Claire Seaman and Richard Bent

Introduction

Corporate citizenship has been defined in many ways, but most definitions include the idea that corporations, businesses, or business-like organisations have a degree of social responsibility, that often includes a responsibility to the families of their employees. Theories that map the traditional territory of corporate social responsibility (Garriga and Melé, 2004) have developed theories in this area, but a general definition is that corporate citizenship refers to a company's responsibilities toward society. The goal is to produce higher standards of living and quality of life for the communities that surround them and still maintain profitability for stakeholders, but this definition raises several questions around who the stakeholders are and to what extent short-term profit and longer-term (for example, environmental) benefits co-exist. Whilst there has been some discussion of stakeholders in the literature, in terms of employees, customers and indeed those who live in the vicinity of the business premises, far less attention has been paid to the scenario where the family is an integral part of the business (McIntosh *et al.*, 1998). This gap within the literature is the focus of this chapter.

Family businesses are astonishingly numerous, often under-researched and yet substantively involved in corporate citizenship, sometimes via formalized routes that include philanthropy and community engagement, but also through their business practices and approaches to corporate social responsibility. Family business is also a relatively young field of research and one that has been, to some extent, bedevilled by definitional debates. Whilst definitions are important, there is a wider issue around family values that may be linked to the corporate citizenship debate. Where one family are substantively involved in a business – whether through ownership, leadership, or management or indeed a blend of these three factors – the values of one family are more likely to influence business behaviour. If we accept that values play a role in business, this concentration of the values of one family within family businesses becomes important. This does not mean, however, that family

DOI: 10.4324/9780429281228-9

businesses universally behave better than their corporate cousins. Rather, for better or worse, the family values may be more likely to influence business behaviour and thus corporate citizenship. Further, in a UK context, the influence of family on business is somewhat obscured by the way business statistics are compiled. Statistics are often collected in the context of business size of the sector of operation, rather than tracking the ownership patterns. Robust research indicates that 65–80% of businesses worldwide could be classified, by various the definitions, as family businesses (Seaman *et al.*, 2018) and it is unlikely that the UK varies from this pattern. Robust statistics may be scarce, but it remains a reasonable conclusion that family businesses are very numerous, have considerable economic importance and may contain a concentration of values that influence business behaviour. Attempts to place corporate citizenship within the literature that looks at business-society relations have not been altogether successful (Maten and Krane, 2005) and one reason may be that by overlooking the often less visible family dimension one driving force is, to some extent, overlooked.

In this chapter, we set out why family businesses are important and highlight some of the roles they play in corporate citizenship. Factoring the family dimension into current corporate citizenship research and the developing potential for new work in this area has the potential to shed light on hitherto unexplored aspects of business behaviour and indeed the embedded working relationships between society and business. The chapter concludes with a model that could form the basis for future research in both qualitative and quantitative methodologies to explore family business corporate citizenship further.

Family Business

The importance of family businesses, in economic terms, has been researched worldwide. Family businesses form a cornerstone of the economies of most developed countries and appear to provide a degree of community and social stability [Poutziouris, 2006; Kets de Vries and Carlock, 2007 pxiii; Institute for Family Business, 2009; Seaman *et al.*, 2018]. Despite their economic importance, family business is a relatively young field of research (Siebels and Knyphausen Aufseb, 2012) and their inclusion into mainstream business thinking in the field of corporate citizenship would be timely. Estimates of the predominance of family business vary, in part due to a lack of definitional clarity, but numerous authors have estimated that somewhere between 65–80% of businesses have families at the core of the business (Collins *et al.*, 2010; Collins *et al.*, 2010; Seaman, 2012, Seaman *et al.*, 2015; 2016). This definitional debate merits further discussion within the family business research community, but in the context of corporate citizenship the definitional challenges are probably less important than the precept that where a family controls a business, the values of that family will contribute to behaviour within that business and hence to corporate citizenship, for good or ill. There is an increasing portfolio of research that suggests that family businesses behave differently from businesses without a substantive family component. Similarly, recent research from the Institute for Family Business indicates that community investments, philanthropy and corporate social responsibility are all expressions of family values and purpose, and that this corporate citizenship behaviour drives social change (Institute for Family Business, 2019). In the context of corporate citizenship, therefore, research that considers how family values influence business decision making makes a useful starting point.

Family and Business Values and Decision Making

Definitions of family and indeed the historical context of 'family' varies widely. Social historians, anthropologists, psychologists and indeed family business scholars have described a wide variety of forms and norms for that entity described as 'family', over a wide variety of historical time periods and social settings (Seaman and Bent, 2017). Indeed, the word family is derived from the Latin 'familia', meaning 'household servants, family' and closely linked to famulus (servant). An operational definition of family, however, has been reached and is quoted by Seaman *et al.* (2018):

> 'a group of individuals linked by blood, living arrangements, marriage or civil partnership who consider themselves to be family, who often choose to spend time together and may live together.'
> (Seaman *et al.*, 2018; adapted from: Family:
> Business Dictionary (2016))

While the historical perspective is interesting, there are also a variety of different contexts where the word family is used in the 21st century, including family in the genetic context, the family as a social construct, the familial analogy in business (Seaman et al, 2014) and indeed varying social structures in countries where religion or tribal affiliation form a core societal unit. This definitional debate is critical, however, because it provides a backdrop to the understanding that family norms and values can only be fairly considered in the context of the time and place in which they are formulated (Bloch and Harrari, 1996; Seaman *et al.*, 2018) and lends weight to the ongoing discussion in the family business literature about the importance of context in family (Seaman and Bent, 2017; Seaman *et al.*, 2018). Family values, in turn, are defined here as:

126 *Claire Seaman and Richard Bent*

'the principles and standards of behaviour, one's judgement of what is important in life'

Oxford English Dictionary, 2016

The importance of family firms and the impact of family values on decision making are important in a general sense, but the focus within this chapter is corporate citizenship. To illustrate the impact family values may have on corporate citizenship, let us consider two aspects of aspects of family business behaviour that are at once very different in scale whilst simultaneously drawing on similar key principles.

1. Family Business Philanthropy

Philanthropy, in a family business context, has been much debated and indeed in 2009 was the subject of a report from the Institute for Family Business that highlighted two aspects: the idea that family business philanthropy and corporate social responsibility in a family business context are on the same continuum (albeit often with different governance arrangements) and the concept that there are three key drivers for family business philanthropy - values, marketing and peer-pressure. The balance between these three values is likely to vary between family businesses and an acknowledgement that family businesses contribute to philanthropy should not be confused with the idea that family businesses are automatically somehow 'better' than their corporate cousins. Rather, and more simply, the family influences the approach to business and philanthropy for better or worse. However, there do appear to be specific benefits that philanthropy brings to a family business that probably do not apply in the corporate context. Many of the family businesses interviewed by the Institute for Family business in 2009 spoke of philanthropy as one way in which members of the family who do not work in the business remain engaged with the overarching family aims and goals. This is a key differentiator because, if we accept that a family business often has a range of family and business goals that are strategically intertwined (Hall, 2002; Fletcher, 2002), the extent to which philanthropy may be seen as carrying a 'local good' may be much higher in a family business context. Anecdotally, several examples present: from the trusts established by families such as Sainsbury, Wolfson and Laing to more local examples such as the Mickel Fund, the importance of 'giving back' engenders itself as an inherent part of their mission, usefully encapsulated by the Mission Statement from the Mickel Trust itself:

'The Mickel Fund is a Registered Scottish Charitable Trust, founded by Douglas W Mickel in the 1970s, with the sole purpose of improving the lives of others through charitable donations in and around Scotland, and where possible on a global scale'.

http://www.mickelfund.org.uk/

Such examples highlight the perceived importance of corporate citizenship, but do not necessarily enhance critical understanding and hence serve as a useful illustration of the need for further research. Examples from both China and the USA highlight the importance of philanthropy in society and indeed the social and philosophical context within which philanthropy is actioned (Susanto and Susanto, 2013; Felio and Botero, 2016). The role of philanthropy and family values is also a major topic in the research and advisory writing around the family business and wealth transition (Williams and Preisser, 2003) but the impact of the family values on the design and implementation of major family philanthropy remains an area for future research (Seaman *et al.*, 2018).

2. Family Businesses and Community Engagement

The distinction between philanthropy and community engagement, also referred to in places as corporate community engagement or corporate community involvement or indeed corporate community investment, is often somewhat artificial, but where philanthropy generally refers to monitory gifting, community engagement is often on a much smaller scale. This does not imply that community engagement is less important: the local business that supports the local children's football team plays a role commensurate with the business size and contributes to social and community cohesion in a very distinct way. The evidence suggests, however, that family businesses are more likely to engage than their non-family run equivalents (Cennamo *et al.*, 2012), but research is limited, and the area would merit further study. Further, one of the challenges when considering the role family businesses play in community engagement is that it is sometimes what the business chooses not to do that may be most important. Research in this area is scarce, but the reluctance of many family businesses to undertake a major geographical relocation is reasonably well-documented and a useful example, perhaps best illustrated in rural areas. Major inward investment and the decisions made by corporate businesses on re-location are often influenced by aspects of infrastructure such as transport links. Within rural communities, a family business may grow and stay in the local area despite its relative geographic remoteness and will often bring benefits in terms of community engagement alongside the employment benefits. Again, the evidence is often anecdotal, but the use of the family land or physical resources associated with the business for local events such as Highland Games or local fairs provide obvious examples.

We should be wary, however, of the lessons we draw from history, here. Historically, small businesses usually started within their local community, and this is where they build their reputation and ties that contribute to community engagement. Globalization and the development of the internet, however, have contributed to a world where customers may lie far from home from the very earliest days of the business and for some businesses this has heralded a fundamental shift in what is meant by 'community'. An illustration, from a UK context, would be the relative decline of regional food retailing in a business environment where there are national/global players and niche specialists but in practice few mid-range chains. Community, we should highlight, may exist in physical form or via virtual reality and probably means very different things to different businesses.

The Mediating Role of Family Values in Decision Making

If family values influence corporate citizenship, they do so via the decision-making process that controls what a business chooses to do or indeed to avoid. Classic, rational financial decision making involves a limited number of actors, who have the information required to make decisions and who act as a manager focused on the business aspects of the decision to be made. This 'rational' behaviour is an assumption within current financial models, drawing on economic theory, which are used by financial institutions to make assessments of firm performance. As the outcome of decisions tends to vary depending on many factors, the quality of decision making is seen as a mechanism that allows participants to simplify the appraisal of potential financial impact and allows investors to make long-term commitments that are essential to economic growth and stability by basing decisions upon expected rather than observed assumptions on behaviour. The issue is of course that in many family firms' financial decisions are not made following the same rationale, methodologies, techniques, or even considering the same type of assumptions and/or variables (Seaman *et al.*, 2018). Smaller family businesses, those that are under the management and control of their founders, by definition will be more likely to be constantly straddling both household and business considerations when making financial decisions (Figure 8.1).

The purpose of this model is to develop a research agenda for corporate citizenship research within family businesses. Several potential mediating variables are identified from the literature that would merit investigation in further and empirical research. Similarly, the potential for a two-way effect between, for example, corporate citizenship activity and community cohesion is noted and would merit further research from at least two viewpoints: it is likely, for example, that community engagement is stronger when economic success is relatively stable, but it is also possible to find examples where difficult times and a need to 'pull together' drive community cohesion when economic stability is threatened. Developing a greater understanding of the way businesses operate within their host communities would allow patterns of engagement to be better understood and would strengthen our understanding of how businesses influence the community for good or ill.

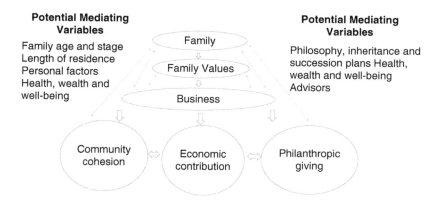

Figure 8.1 Modelling Corporate Citizenship.

Conclusions

The role of family businesses in philanthropy and community engagement should not, over-shadow a more general point, however. Family businesses are the most numerous forms of businesses and form the backbone of economies and communities worldwide (Seaman, 2012, 2013). It is as difficult to generalize about family businesses as it is to generalize about the business community in general, but the distinction between wholly-family-owned businesses and businesses that have made the jump to a corporate identity is worth highlighting. Families can choose or develop their values to some extent (for better or worse). Where a business is wholly or very largely family-owned, therefore, family values can exhibit an influence with some degree of impunity. A corporation, by contrast, has a legal responsibility to its shareholders to generate profits in most cultures. This distinction will probably influence business behaviour but does not detract from the importance of family business in our thinking around corporate citizenship. Two aspects emphasize the general importance of family businesses in corporate citizenship, Research evidence from the United States of America suggests that the wording of family business mission statements carries a more 'socially responsible' message than that of their corporate cousins (Blodget et al., 2011). Alongside evidence that the approach of family business to corporate social responsibility varies (Deniz and Suarez, 2005), this might reasonably suggest that their approaches to corporate citizenship should be explored in greater depth. The weight of numbers also suggests that the impact of family businesses on corporate citizenship merits research. This chapter touches on the very heart of definitions of corporate citizenship. If we think of 'corporate' as meaning only those businesses without a significant family component, we overlook most

130 Claire Seaman and Richard Bent

businesses worldwide. Families run businesses and are engaged in the full spectrum of business behaviour. Whilst they undoubtedly contribute to major philanthropic programmes and indeed community engagement, they convey far more in terms of benefits and challenges in terms of their day-to-day business behaviour. Family businesses also provide a fertile ground for future business leaders to develop their business values and expertise, highlighted by recent work on business integrity (Seaman and Bent, 2017). A key facet of this debate, however, remains the lack of research that considers family business in the context of corporate citizenship. Considering family values (Seaman and Bent, 2017) highlighted that while family values were important, this should not be taken to mean that family values were always positive. Rather, where a business was run by several different members of the same family, the importance of family values may become concentrated for better or worse. The notion that family businesses provide a concentration and potentially intensification of values within a business has a direct link to corporate citizenship, because the concentration of values may make values-based action more likely. Further, the relatively informal governance and decision-making mechanisms in many family businesses may lend themselves to relatively quick decision making around, for example, community engagement or support for local events. Attempts to capture corporate citizenship, such as the 'Civic 50' list produced by the Conference Board (2015), begin to highlight the extent of current engagement but there is more that can be done in the area and indeed anecdotal evidence suggests there is more to be captured (Cater et al., 2015; Garcia et al., 2016).

The relative lack of research in many areas associated with corporate citizenship within the family business community is striking, although perhaps less surprising given the relatively young nature of family business as a research area. Further exploratory and empirical research to explore their role in corporate citizenship is overdue, which should include the development of a research agenda. The hallmark of strong, scientific research is the development of a body of knowledge derived from focused, empirical projects and this development should form the next stage for the development of the family business and corporate citizenship agenda.

In developing a research agenda around family business and corporate citizenship, therefore, we think about where this focused approach might be applied. One obvious area is around approaches to corporate citizenship by family businesses in different sectors, geographic areas and indeed businesses of very different sizes and degrees of professionalization. From the crofting communities of the Scottish Highlands to minority ethnic business communities and to substantive businesses with formalized decision making and corporate social responsibility functions across the globe, culture and community values are likely to influence corporate citizenship behaviours and merit attention.

Acknowledgement

Some of the ideas presented in this chapter originally appeared as a 'Turning Point' piece in the journal in the Journal of Corporate Citizenship. Our thanks go to the editorial team for permission to re-develop the ideas here. The full reference for this work is:

Seaman, C. and Bent, R. (2017) Turning Point: Factoring the Family into Corporate Citizenship. *The Journal of Corporate Citizenship*, No. 65(March 2017), pp. 6-11. 10.9774/GLEAF.4700.2017.ma.00003.

References

Blodget, M.S., Dumas, C. and Zanzi, A. (2011) 'Emerging trends in global ethics: A comparative study of U.S. and international family business values', *Journal of Business Ethics*, 99, pp. 29–38.

Cater, C., Collins, L.A. and Brent, D.B. (2015) 'Family firm engagement in fair trade business models'. United States Association for Small Business and Entrepreneurship. Conference Proceedings; Boca Raton, pp. R1–R23. Boca Raton: United States Association for Small Business and Entrepreneurship.

Cennamo, C. *et al.* (2012) 'Socioemotional wealth and proactive stakeholder engagement: Why family-controlled firms care more about their stakeholders', *Entrepreneurship Theory and Practice*, 36, pp. 1153–1173 10.1111/j.1540-6520. 2012.00543.x.

Collins, L. and O'Regan, N. (2010) 'The evolving field of family business', *Journal of Family Business Management*, 1(1), pp. 5–13. ISSN 2043-6238.

Collins, L. *et al.* (2010) 'Strategic thinking in family businesses', *Strategic Change*, 19(1–2), pp. 57–76. ISSN 1086-1718.

Campopiano, G., De Massis, A. and Chirico, F. (2014). 'Ownership and management firm philanthropy in small- and medium-sized family firms: The effects of family involvement in ownership and management', *Family Business Review*, 27(24), pp. 4 10.1177/0894486514538450.

Deniz, M. de la Cruz and Suarez, M.K.C. (2005) 'Corporate social responsibility and family business in Spain', *Journal of Business Ethics*, 56, pp. 27–41

Felio, N. and Botero, I. (2016) 'Philanthropy in family enterprises: A review of literature', *Family Business Review 2016*, 29(1), pp. 121–141.

Fletcher, D. (2002) *Understanding the small family business. Routledge studies in small business*. London and New York: Taylor and Francis Group.

Garcia, M.E. *et al.* (2016) 'Toolkit of resources for engaging families and the community as partners in education. Part 1: Building an understanding of family and community engagement', *REL*, pp. 2016–2148 https://eric.ed.gov/?id= ED569110.

Garriga, E. and Melé, D. (2004) 'Corporate social responsibility theories: Mapping the territory', *Journal of Business Ethics*, 53(1), pp. 51–71.

132 Claire Seaman and Richard Bent

Hall, A. (2002) 'Towards an understanding of strategy processes in small family business', in Fletcher D.E. (ed.), *Understanding the small family business*. Routledge studies in small business. London and New York: Taylor and Francis Group.

Institute for Family Business (2009) 'Natural philanthropists: Findings of the family business philanthropy and social responsibility inquiry'. http://www.cgap.org.uk/uploads/natural-philanthropists.pdf.

Institute for Family Business (2019) *Social Impact in 100-year Family Businesses*. Ed. D. Jaffe https://www.ifb.org.uk/news/news/social-impact-in-hundred-year-family-businesses/.

Kets de Vries, M.F.R. and Carlock, R.S. (2007) *Family business on the couch*. London: Wiley and Sons.

Maten, D. and Krane, A. (2005) 'Corporate citizenship: Toward an extended theoretical conceptualisation', *Academy of Management Review*, 30(1), pp. 166–179

McIntosh, M. *et al.* (1998) *Corporate citizenship: Successful strategies for responsible companies*. London, UK: Pitman Publishing.

Poutziouris, Z.P. (2006) 'The structure and performance of the UK family business PLC economy', in Poutziouris P.Z., Smyrnios K.X. and Klein S.B. (eds.), *Handbook of Research on Family Businesses*. Cheltenham, UK: Edward Elgar.

Seaman, C., Silva, M. and Bent, R. (2018) 'Family values: Influencers in the development of financial and non-financial dynamics in family firms', in Memili E. and Dibrell C. (eds.), *The Palgrave handbook of heterogeneity among family firms*. Palgrave Macmillan. https://www.palgrave.com/us/book/9783319776750#aboutBook.

Seaman, C. and Bent, R. (2017) 'The role of family values in the integrity of family business', in Orlitzky M. and Monga Manjit (eds.), *Facets of integrity in business and management*. Routledge.

Seaman, C., Bent, R. and Unis, A. (2016) 'The role of context. South Asian family firms in Scotland and the succession paradox ', *International Journal of Management Practice, Special Issue on 'The Role of Context in Family Firms'*, 9(4), pp. 433–437.

Seaman, C., Bent, R. and Unis, A. (2015) 'The future of family entrepreneurship: Family culture', *Education and Entrepreneurial Intent in Scottish Pakistani Communities. Futures. Special Issue on the Futures of Family Entrepreneurship*. Editors: K. Randerson, A. Fayolle and C. Bettinelli. http://www.sciencedirect.com/science/article/pii/S0016328715300458.

Seaman, C. (2013) 'The invisible bedrock: Business families, networks and the creation of entrepreneurial space', *World Review of Entrepreneurship, Management and Sustainable Development*, 9(1), pp. 101–113. ISSN 1746-0573.

Seaman, C. (2012) 'The invisible bedrock: Four constructs of family business space', *World Review of Entrepreneurship, Management and Sustainable Development*, 8(3), pp. 297–307. ISSN 1746-0573.

Siebels, J.F. and Knyphausen Aufseb, D.Z. (2012) 'A review of theory in family business research: The implication for corporate governance', *International Journal of Management Reviews*, 14, pp. 280–304.

Susanto, A.B. and Susanto, P. (2013) *The dragon network. Inside stories of the most successful chinese family businesses*. Singapore: John Wiley Press.

Williams, R. and Preisser, V. (2003) *Preparing Heirs: Five steps to a successful transition of family weath and values*. California: Robert D. Reed Publishers.

Index

Note: Italicized and bold page numbers refer to figures and tables. Page numbers followed by "n" refer to notes.

ABN AMRO project 94
agency theory 37
Aguinis, H. 16, 56
Allahabad Bank 92
Alonso-Almeida, M.D.M. 58
Altman, B. 117
altruism 16, 17
anchored power 45–46, **54**
Aristotle 88
assertiveness 88
Astrachan, C. 24

Bank of Baroda 95
Barnard, C. 9
Baxter, J. 102
Belcher, A. 102
Bernhard, F. **15**
BFCB *see* business family citizenship behaviour (BFCB)
Binz Astrachan, C. 8, **15**, 16, 74
Birla, A. 90
Birla, G.D. 93
Block, J. H. **15**, 71, 74
Bombay Plan 93
Brammer, S. 12
Britannia Biscuits 95
business communities 88–90; traditions of philanthropy across 90–94
business family citizenship behaviour (BFCB) 17–25; drivers of 19–22, *23*; outcomes 22, 24–25; types of **20**
business opportunity 119

Calhoun, C. 111
Campopiano, G. 9, **15**

capitalism 87, 88, 96
Carroll, A.B. 10
Cennamo, C. **15**
Chiaburu, D.S. 20
citizens, responsibilities of 9
citizenship behaviours 9–14; business family 17–25, **20**, *23*; dimensionality of 8, 9; employee 12, 14; enterprise/corporate 17; individual 17; organizational 8, 10, *11*, 14, 16, 18, 21–22
citizenship behaviours, in family enterprises 8–28, *11*, *13*, **15**; future research, directions for 27–28; interconnections at multiple levels of analysis 25–27; multi-level nature of 16–17
civic virtue 16
civil society 1
Coleman, G. 103–105, **106**, 108
Commission of European Communities (EC) 59
community engagement 5; family business and 127–128
Company Act 2013 86, 98
conscientiousness 16
corporate citizenship 1–6, 8, 17, 133; antecedents and influences of 70–81; citizen of, constructing 111–112; definition of 10, 70, 104; drivers and outcomes of *13*; effects on organizational performance 12; external 12; family values, role of 73; feminism and 105–111; founder's role 74; four sides of

134 *Index*

10–11; future research directions 78–80, **80–81**; gender and 102–112; global 118; implications of 78–80; intergenerational aspirations 73–74; internal 12; limitations of 78–80; in Medkit 75–77, 78; modelling *129*; socioemotional wealth 74
corporate ethics 10
corporate social responsibility (CSR) 2–4, 10, 12, 16, 18, 94, 98–100, 114; definition of 36, 59; perceptions and trust in organization 60–61; Ramadan package as 56–64; in small-scaled hospitality companies 57–58; sustainability in historic family firms 34, 36–37, 39, 40, 42, 45, 48, 49
courtesy 16
Crane, A. 104
Cruz, C. **15**
CSR *see* corporate social responsibility (CSR)
Cui, V. **15**
Cummings, L.L. 16, 18, 28n1

DCM (Delhi Cloth and General Mills Company) 95
Dharma 87–88
Dilip Kumar Lakhi 94

economy 86–88
embedded ethics 42–43, 53
employee citizenship behaviour 12, 14
equality 107
equity 107
Erez, A. 16

family, definition of 4, 125
family business 1–6, 124–125; and community engagement 127–128; philanthropy 126–127
family cohesion 22
family enterprises, citizenship behaviours in 8–28, *11*, *13*, **15**; business family citizenship behaviour 17–25, **20**, *23*; future research, directions for 27–28; interconnections at multiple levels of analysis 25–27; multi-level nature of 16–17
family-owned businesses' corporate citizenship: business opportunity 119; financial and cost management systems, impact of 114–120; global

corporate citizenship 118; methodology 116; partnership society 119–120; stakeholder relationship 118–119; transformation 119
family ownership 3, 39
family values 125–126; in decision making, mediating role of 128; definition of 4; role of 5
feminism: and corporate citizenship 105–111; gender reform 105, 107
feminist discourse 104–111, **106**
Ferrel, O. 104
Font, X. 58
Foreign Exchange Management Act of 1973 95
Frederick, W. 37–39, 50–51

Gandhi, M. 93
Garay, L. 58
gender 5; and corporate citizenship 102–112; equality 103; rebellion 109–111; reform feminism 105, 107; resistance 111; revolution 110
GKN (Guest, Keen and Williams) 95
Glavas, A. 16, 56
Global Compact U.N principles 43
global corporate citizenship 118
Golder, B. 110
governance 94–98
Graham, J.W. 9–10
grounded stewardship 46, **54**
group loyalty 87
Guba, E.G. 49

Hamied, K.A. 95
harmony 88
Herbik, P.A. 21
Hundi system 92, 95

IKEA 97
Ilies, R. 21
implicit mutual interest 44–45, **53–54**
Institute for Family Business 125
intergenerational aspirations 73–74
isomorphism 90

Jagat Seth 92
Jamnalal Bajaj 93
Johnson, D.E. 16

Kanya Daan Trust 91
Katz, D. 9

Index   135

Kellermanns, F.W. **15**
Kim, K. **15**
Kirloskar, L. 95
Kreiner, G.E. 27

Labelle, R. **15**
Laws of Manu 88
Lean, E. 21
learning by doing 43–44, **53**
Le Breton-Miller, I. 8
LePine, J.A. 16, 20
limited shareholder pressure, in family firms 72–73
Lin, C.P. 12
Lincoln, Y.S. 49
loyalty 9

Madison, K. **15**
Maignan, I. 104
Marler, L.E. **15**
Marques, P. **15**
Martin Burns 95
Matherne, C. **15**
Matten, D. 104
McLarty, B.D. **15**
McLean Parks, J. 16, 18, 28n1
Medkit: corporate citizenship in 75–77, 78
Metal Box 95
Mickel Trust: Mission Statement 126
Miller, D. 8
Millington, A. 12
Mittal, S. **15**
Moi, T. 110
Morgeson, F.P. 21

Nahrgang, J.D. 21
natural moral sense 46–47, **54–55**
Nehru, J. 93
Nietzche, F. 88
Njite, D. 58

obedience 9
OCB-I see organizational citizenship behaviour, individuals (OCB-I)
OCB-O see organizational citizenship behaviour, organization (OCB-O)
OCBs see organizational citizenship behaviours (OCBs)
O'Driscoll, M.P. **15**
Olson, D.H. 22
organizational citizenship behaviour, individuals (OCB-I) 10

organizational citizenship behaviour, organization (OCB-O) 10
organizational citizenship behaviours (OCBs) 10, 14, 18, 21–22; definition of 61; dimensions of 16; nomological network *11*

participation 9
partnership society 119–120
Patel, V. 93
Pearce, C.L. 21
perceived corporate sincerity, moderating role of 62–63
philanthropy 5; across business communities, traditions of 90–94; family business 126–127
Podsakoff, P.M. 20
power aggrandizement, barriers to 50–51
Protestant Ethics 89
Punjab National Bank 92, 95
PWC 3

Ramadan package 4; conceptual model *59*; and CSR perceptions 59–60; employees returns on 56–64; hypothesis development 57; literature review 57
Ramos, H.M. **15**
rationality 87
Rayton, B. 12
Rhou, Y. 57
rule of reciprocity 60

Seaman, C. 16, 28n2
sex 104–111
sexual harassment 108
Singal, M. 57, 58
Singh, S. **15**
SIT see social identity theory (SIT)
Smith, N. 118
social corporate responsibility 104
social exchange theory 60
social identity, in family businesses 35–36
social identity theory (SIT) 35
social information processing theory 26
social life 87
society 86–88
socioemotional wealth 74; model 70
sportsmanship 16
stakeholder relationship 118–119

136 *Index*

Stanley, L.J. **15**
state 86–88
Sundaramurthy, C. 27
sustainability, in historic family firms 34–51; anchored power 45–46, **54**; barriers to power aggrandizement 50–51; data structure **41**; embedded ethics 42–43, **53**; findings 41–42; grounded, systemic continuity 49–50; grounded stewardship 46; guardians of 47–48, **55**; implicit mutual interest 44–45, **53–54**; learning by doing 43–44, **53**; limits of 51; methods 39–41; natural moral sense 46–47, **54–55**; tacitness 49–50; values in business, framework of 36–39

tacitness 49–50
TBL *see* Triple Bottom Line Reporting (TBL)

team level citizenship 18
Triple Bottom Line Reporting (TBL) 90
trust in organization: CSR perceptions and 60–61; mediating effect of 61–62; organizational citizenship behaviour and 61

values: in business, framework of 36–39; ecologizing 37, 38; economizing 37, 38; family 4, 5, 125–126; family, role of 73; tacit 43
Van Dyne, L. 16, 18, 20, 28n1
Vidaver-Cohen, D. 117

Waddock, S. 118
Wagner, M. **15**, 71, 74
Weber, M. 89
welfare state model 78
White, D.W. 21

Milton Keynes UK
Ingram Content Group UK Ltd.
UKHW031503071224
451979UK00020B/213